he New York Hilton, New York, New York The Hampshire House Hotel, New
York, New York The Omni, Atlanta, Georgia The Om[illegible] The
Loew's Hotel, Monte Carlo, Monaco Le Cirque Restaurant, Mayfair House,
ork Top of the Park Restaurant, One Gulf & Western Plaza, New York, New
s, New York, New York El Morocco, New York, New York Max's Steak House,
The Grotto Restaurant, The Omni, Miami, Florida Bank AmeriLease of New
ille, New York, New York Bank AmeriLease of Cleveland, Ohio Peoples Bank
pi Bank of Forest, Forest, Mississippi First Citizens National Bank, Tupelo,
rk, New York Revlon at the General Motors Building, New York, New York
Georgia Rockwell International, Richardson, Texas Loral Corporation, New
ling, Pittsburgh, Pennsylvania Wallace, Dixon, & Dover, Little Rock, Arkansas
haeuser, Inc., Hot Springs, Arkansas Orbit Valve International, Little Rock,
nt Transport, Lowell, Arkansas George's, Inc., Springdale, Arkansas Conway
Arkansas Clay County Medical Center, West Point, Mississippi Doctors
terans Admin. Hospital, Little Rock, Arkansas [illegible] Memorial Hospital,
inistration Spinal Cord Injury Unit, Memphis, Tennessee Freeway Medical
ker County Medical Center, Jasper, Alabama Good Shepherd Ecumenical
Arkansas College at Batesville, Arkansas C.W. Post College, Brookville, New
ary School, Conway, Arkansas Julia Lee Moore Elementary School, Conway,
na The Shelter Rock Jewish Center, Roslyn, New York First Baptist Church,
Church of the Nazarene, Little Rock, Ark[illegible] Baptist Church, Conway,
nway, Arkansas The Chapel, Human Development Center, Conway, Arkansas
White Plains, New York Shelter Rock Country Club, Long Island, New York
Reception Room with Mrs. Jacqueline Kennedy [illegible] Governor's Mansion,
sda, Maryland Bridgehampton, Long Island, New York Fairbanks Ranch,
k, New York 817 Fifth Avenue, New York, New York 820 Fifth Avenue, New
, New York 936 Fifth Avenue, New York, New York 1070 Fifth Avenue, New
rk, New York 755 Park Avenue, New York, New York 784 Park Avenue, New
ork, New York 1125 Park Avenue, New York, New York The Trump Towers,
Number 1 Sutton Place, New York, New York Number 4 Sutton Place, New
necticut Helsinki, Finland Hyannis Port, Massachusetts Jakarta, Indonesia
Memphis, Tennessee Middleburg, Virginia Montego Bay, Jamaica Rancho
t Sun Valley, Idaho Vail, Colorado Washington, D.C., Virginia Westchester
P's Place, Little Rock, Arkansas Feinsteins, Little Rock, Arkansas Adrienne
's, Little Rock, Arkansas Signatures by BP, Little Rock, Arkansas Strawberry
ork and Stamford, Connecticut The Carlyle Hotel, New York, New York

TO HELEN WALKER,

MAY THIS BOOK ADD
TO THE JOY IN YOUR HOME.

YOU ARE LOVED!
GEORGE

Silent Witness

The Language of Your Home

Silent Witness

The Language of Your Home

BY GEORG ANDERSEN, ASID
WITH JAMES McALISTER

TYNDALE HOUSE PUBLISHERS, INC.
WHEATON, ILLINOIS

Visit Tyndale's exciting Web site at www.tyndale.com
Georg Andersen's Web site is www.georgandersen.com

Published by Tyndale House Publishers, Inc. Wheaton, IL

ISBN 0-8423-3533-1

Printed in the United States of America

03 02 01 00 99
5 4 3 2 1

DEDICATION

I dedicate this book to Jenny, Amy, our grandson Calvin Wesley—and to all created by God with special needs—as well as to our grandson Kent Edward, who is ever so special to us and to his Creator.

ACKNOWLEDGMENTS

This book extols the virtue of keeping silent . . . letting the *spirit* of the home speak to all who enter.

The words I'm using in these first pages are an attempt to explain my gratitude for having been cheered on by so many. At the top of the list of those whose support I've valued is my wife, Annabelle. Next, Bill and Gloria Gaither, who planted the thought and gave permission to use "Silent Witness" as the title for the book.

My friend Jim Warren of Moody Broadcasting in Chicago gave me insights through his listening audience that people do long to be creative and need to *use* their homes.

Ruth Graham has long encouraged Annabelle and me and our three children to make no excuse for the home God has so graciously provided for us.

My friend and writer James McAlister, with the insightful counsel and encouragement of his wife, Mary, gave breath and life to what I so very much wanted to share with those longing to use their homes to impart love and care for others.

To Matthew A. Price, my thanks for steering me to Tyndale House, where Tammy Faxel, Gloria Keibler, Erin Keeley, Jacki Vietmeier, and Annette Taroli immediately took ownership of this project.

Table of Contents

A NOTE ABOUT ANNABELLE

Without Annabelle's giving heart, the doors of our home would never be opened as they are through these pages. An intensely private person, Annabelle has the ability to "be there" for anyone who needs shelter, food, or an encouraging ear.

I polled our immediate family and friends, and these are the words they used to describe my bride of almost thirty-five years:

- Constant nurturer
- Subtle peacemaker
- A sweet, gentle spirit
- An angel here on earth
- Empathetic . . . and lives it
- Willing to grow and be taught
- Supportive
- A great listener
- A friend through thick and thin
- Fiercely loyal
- Devoted to family and friends
- Authentic, candid, grounded
- A perfect example of probity
- A lot of fun
- She replenishes herself daily in God's well of strength, mercy, and tenderness . . . and is then generous enough to pour out from her spirit into each of us who knows her.

It is my sincere hope that you will see and "hear" some of these descriptions of Annabelle loudly and clearly as God reveals himself to you as a result of her willingness to share the "language of our home" with you.

George

GEORG ANDERSEN

LETTERS OF ENDORSEMENT

No matter what the size of one's home, it can and should be a welcoming place. Whether a cottage or a mansion, if loving hearts live there, it will show in the family pictures, the old loved books, and the bits and pieces of treasures accumulated through the years. . . .

I think Georg Andersen has captured beautifully the things that make a home where a welcome always greets you. . . . Theirs is a home and not just a house—a home that is lived in and loved and where guests are made to feel especially welcome. As I look through the book, I get ideas for a few more finishing touches on our home.

You will find this book helpful and practical as you plan for a new home or simply wish to make the place where you live one that will be a pleasure to others as well as to you and your family.

RUTH GRAHAM

No matter where I've gone . . . one constant has remained true over the years: My heart beats faster when it is time to go home.

This book is a celebration of home, written by a man who is eminently qualified to speak on the subject. Most people know Georg Andersen because of his achievements in the field of interior design. Indeed, the professional accolades are well deserved, as anyone who has visited a building that's been changed by his creative vision can attest. But for those who have been privileged to be guests in Georg and Annabelle's home, those professional accomplishments fade into the background, lost amidst the splendor and beauty of both the surroundings and the hearts of the family who lives there.

It has been often said that "home is where the heart is." Perhaps the better statement is that "home reveals where the heart is.". . .

May the truths you glean from these pages lead you further down the pathway toward a legacy of home that endures from generation to generation.

STEVE SCHALL
PRESIDENT
K-LIFE, INC.

"Achieving gracious living that enriches your family, your guests, and you" is a cause that has been championed frequently by Georg Andersen during his appearances over the years as a guest on Moody Broadcasting Network's *Prime Time America*. As the host and director of this national radio magazine, I have observed Georg's gracious and practical help given to the many listeners who called him for advice—a variety of listeners whose homes may vary from a seven-figure price tag to . . . a small apartment or house trailer.

His unique approach to decorating and furnishing one's home is biblically based and reminds us of the scriptural injunction to begin one's ministry at their "Jerusalem," and from there to move outward. Georg reminds us that how we treat our homes is not to be considered a trivial matter; he insists that decorating and furnishing our homes in a manner that reflects the Lord and our individuality is significant for the emotional and spiritual well-being of our families, our guests, and ourselves.

Georg Andersen, in his appearances on *Prime Time America* over the past several years, has "freed up" many of the listeners . . . to decorate with the color and style and imagination that reflect their own tastes.

On a personal basis, my wife, Jean, and I can testify to the wonderful sense of peace and renewal we experienced as guests in this Adamsbrooke address from which Georg and Annabelle minister. What he speaks about, they live! While they obviously had lovely furnishings, simplicity and grace were always present; it was obvious they were not out to impress us but rather to make us comfortable and to meet our needs. Their Spirit-generated love, plus the warmth of their comfortable refuge, had an unmistakable nurturing effect on us; through them we experienced the presence of the Lord. These principles work!

I thank God for our teacher and loving brother Georg Andersen and his track record of generously helping the rest of us make the best of whatever home ministry potential is ours. We reap the benefit of thirty-five years of experience from a man who combines true professionalism with a practicality that comes from a genuine heart's desire to serve God and to help us enjoy our homes and more richly bless others who visit. Enjoy!

JIM WARREN
HOST/EXECUTIVE PRODUCER
PRIME TIME AMERICA
MOODY BROADCASTING NETWORK

Many Christians dream and even sing of someday "living in a mansion." In July 1996, my family and I went from living in a regular home to a mansion—the governor's mansion of Arkansas. Such a move marked quite an adjustment from the life Janet and I had begun when we married in May 1974 as college students and lived in a duplex apartment for forty dollars a month.

Georg Andersen helped us make the mansion a home. Frankly, he did more than that. He enabled us to survive a difficult first year as the first family of Arkansas by being our friend, our designer, our prayer partner, and, most recently, a member of the Governor's Mansion Commission. . . . He helped us make the family quarters uniquely ours and gave our children a sense of ownership and belonging in an environment where privacy doesn't exist and life and schedules are often in the hands of others. . . .

The fact that he was willing to be of assistance to his adopted home state and its new governor and first lady proved to be more than an adventure in decorating. It was a spiritual pilgrimage for us as we were led by this godly servant into territories of taste and touch beyond our background as a pastor and pastor's wife. . . .

Georg and Annabelle have not merely built and decorated a dwelling; they have created a Christ-centered retreat that exudes elegance without opulence, and dignity that is complemented by wonderful human warmth and character.

As Georg and Annabelle introduce their home to you in the pages of this wonderful book, you will soon discover that you are being invited to more than an "open house." It is instead an "open heart" of grace and charm that is at the core of their lives. You will enjoy the reading, learn much about hospitality and creating an environment of welcome, and come to treasure your new friendship with two wonderful people, Georg and Annabelle Andersen.

MIKE HUCKABEE
GOVERNOR
STATE OF ARKANSAS

INTRODUCTION

While there are other books on the subject of interior decorating, we are not aware of any that specifically address enhancing the inherent "witness" of the home.

Many Christians fail to effectively employ one of their greatest resources to influence others for Christ—their home. That's not the way it should be, and with the encouragement of this book, that's not the way it has to be.

Silent Witness: The Language of Your Home will describe how any home—your home included—can become effective, aesthetically pleasing, and hospitable. But more importantly, it will examine what our homes say about our beliefs, priorities, and purpose in life. These are the words of silent witness that influence others.

Aesthetically appealing photographs with substantial captions illustrate Mr. Andersen's years of experience in design and provide meaningful content even for browsers. But to more serious students, the book will be a guide to help them discover the underlying basis and motivations for the concepts presented through the individual "words" of silent witness from their home.

This book follows Mr. Andersen's previous book, *Interior Decorating: A Reflection of the Creator's Design* (Bethany House).

Veteran photographer Rick Taylor of Atlanta—whose clients include national home magazines and numerous large companies—has prepared (with a few exceptions, as noted) the photographs.

The Importance of Home

CHAPTER 1

TIME'S LONG AND FLOWING RIVER

IN TIME'S LONG AND FLOWING RIVER,
SWEPT ALONG, I CANNOT ROAM—
CONTEMPLATE MY CIRCUMSTANCES—
AS IT TAKES ME SURELY HOME.

MANY TIMES I'VE LONGED TO LINGER,
SPEND A WHILE OUTSIDE ITS FLOW;
LET THE TRIALS OF LIFE SLIP BY ME,
BUT I'M DRAWN ALONG IN TOW.

LOOKING AT MY FRIENDS AND FAMILY,
OH, HOW YOUNG THEY SEEM TO BE!
RIVER FLOWS, AND THEY'RE MUCH OLDER;
TIME IS ALSO CHANGING ME.

GENTLE MOMENTS WITH MY CHILDREN;
HOW I THOUGHT THEY'D ALWAYS BE.
LOOK AGAIN, AND ONE IS MISSING!
GONE AHEAD TO WAIT FOR ME.

ERRORS MADE WHEN I WAS YOUNGER
FOLLOW ME AND CAUSE REGRETS.
CAN'T GO BACK, THE RIVER'S FLOWING;
SOMETIMES FEAR WHAT LIES AHEAD.

BUT I HAVE A WATCHFUL PILOT,
ALWAYS KNOWS JUST WHERE WE ARE.
KEEPS US SAFE WITHIN HIS RIVER,
'TIL IT CROSSES HEAVEN'S BAR.[1]

As this poem poignantly reminds us, Christians are a people in transition. We are on a slow but steady journey between two worlds held apart by time. But until we reach the confluence, we are to be about the business of emulating Jesus in our daily walks, integrating and engrafting his character into every aspect of our lives.

The very essence of a home is inexorably bound to the way that life is expressed through it. And the high ground that we hope to claim in this book is to help make that expression a picture of Christ. But more about that in a moment.

Have you ever given much thought to what makes a home? We probably most easily identify with the wood, bricks, stone, and other materials that comprise the structure itself, but who would equate a house with a home?

[1]"Time's Long and Flowing River" © 1997 James McAlister. Used by permission.

Nevertheless, these physical components and the thoughts behind them *say* a lot about the occupants and their activities. Naturally, our homes don't speak with words per se, but they subtly reveal so much: interests and priorities . . . the place God has in our lives . . . our concerns for others . . . the value that we put on our families . . . how we spend our time.

Thus, our homes become "silent witnesses" to the multifaceted work of God in our lives. St. Francis of Assisi succinctly immortalized this concept: "Preach the gospel everywhere; when necessary use words."

Words of silent witness are vitally important, for they affect—by either helping or hindering—our work and influence for the Lord. Perhaps you've been in a home or a business and were immediately struck with the harmony and peace that were there. Or you could have sensed irritation or discontentment or bitterness. You were receiving words of silent witness!

We'll look at a lot of these important words of witness in this book. Just so you don't miss them, they'll be set apart in distinctive type along with some working definitions. Still, we must train our hearts to listen—to our own homes in particular—to see what they are really saying.

FAITH

Visualizing God's plan and responding accordingly

What really makes a "good" home? Much of today's thinking would tell us that affluence and abundance are prerequisites, but Moses provides evidence to the contrary: "It was by faith that Moses left the land of Egypt. He was not afraid of the king. Moses kept right on going because he kept his eyes on the one who is invisible" (Hebrews 11:27).

When Moses forsook Egypt, what did he leave behind? Riches, power, and prestige—the things that many of us struggle to obtain—had all been his. For the next forty years his desert home provided something beyond the trappings of worldly success that the palace could not.

There's a lesson here. If God has appointed you to dwell in a rented room or a lodge in the mountains, then your living conditions should neither cause you to boast nor to be ashamed. Only when Christians have the freedom to honestly believe that God is working through their circumstances can their homes be all that he intends. To the extent that we catch a vision of the potential of the home, our homes will speak of FAITH.

Isn't that what Moses did? He saw a monarch far greater than Pharaoh that compelled him down the path of faith. Can you picture what God can do and wants to do through you and your home, and then act in harmony with that vision? If so, FAITH will speak volumes to others.

In developing such an outlook, we will wrestle with personal priorities. And if the Lord Jesus Christ, his truth, and our family, friends, and guests rank high enough on our lists, then we will focus on meeting others' needs, not impressing people, when we open our homes. FAITH is motivated by the results that we see with the heart, not by the visible hindrances that seem to block the way.

CONTENTMENT

Accepting God's present provision of shelter and clothing as sufficient

Think with me for a moment. Even with the busyness of today's culture, we still spend the bulk of our lives eating, sleeping, and working through the ordinary needs of daily living. Where? In our homes, of course. Consequently, we can't put a price tag on a home that effectively facilitates such lifelong processes.

Still, Christians often feel guilty about investing time, resources, and attention toward the assemblage of their homes. In fact, just the thought of how to begin to establish a *tone* for the home sometimes brings on a paralysis of sorts. As a result, many miss the joy of seeing gifts and ministries developed. Instead of serving as launching pads, their homes become more like anchors.

In all seasons of life, people need to share heartaches and worries along with joys and victories. What better place than in a warm, nonthreatening home? But our tendency is to focus on externals—such as jobs, positions, or possessions—and overlook others' hurts and needs. Thus we can wrongly conclude that others have it made, and we miss the opportunity to really share the deep issues of our hearts. But how good it is to be in a place where the fruit of the Spirit is manifested to everyone!

But FAITH can be thwarted if her handmaid, CONTENTMENT, is not present.

Do you experience CONTENTMENT with your home, or do you expend energy pursuing—either physically or emotionally—something beyond the means that God has provided?

Covetousness is another word for *discontentment,* and it shows up in our choices and inner desires and drives. In the pages that follow, you'll be taking a look at the home God has given us, but you shouldn't long for it or any other. Taken together, FAITH and CONTENTMENT are a source of great gain. They keep us on track by coupling a vision of what can be with a satisfaction that what we have is sufficient in God's divine scheme.

Having been an interior designer for some thirty-five-plus years, one mission in this phase of my life is to help Christians develop homes that are the best they can be. Surprisingly, this doesn't have to mean more "stuff."

Yet most situations are unique enough to spawn a myriad of presumptions that can strangle and confine. Actually, there are really no hard-and-fast rules. If you like things a certain way, who am I to say, "Don't do it"?

The word BOLDNESS has taken a bad rap because of certain pushy types whom we all have had to endure! It should, nonetheless, be in your home's vocabulary. Without it you will be tossed about by every wind of trend that blows through the area.

BOLDNESS

The confidence that neither my words nor my actions are morally offensive to God or to others

If red walls make your soul sing or raspberry gives you the warm fuzzies, then why not? The fear of what others think keeps us from making certain choices. There's certainly a place for good taste, but so much that causes us to hold back in using our homes doesn't really make any difference. A bit of BOLDNESS in moving forward even if everything isn't exactly perfect is what we need.

If we wait until conditions are exactly right before sharing a verbal witness, the Good News will seldom go out. And so it is with our homes. There will always be something that we may be fearful about, but does it *really* matter?

We must remember that people don't come into our homes to look at *things;* they come for a "banquet of the heart." They long to sense the spirit of the home and to enjoy the fellowship that they inwardly desire.

In a word, they are seeking expressions of SINCERITY.

Hearts are touched, not by opulence, but by intent and concern. Having a wonderful home doesn't make others feel wonderful if they are hurting. But all who have been embraced by the depth of love in a home that speaks SINCERITY, however, will depart with lingering thoughts of the incredible experience that has come their way.

Renowned designer Henri Samuel once said, "Good design should convey the *feeling* that a house has always been that way and that no decorator has been a part of it." And while Christians can't base their lives on feelings alone, what our homes "say" is vitally important.

SINCERITY

The genuine, earnest desire to help others without the motive of personal gain

Can you imagine your home as a witness to values, the very values that *you* will pass to future generations? Can you see your home as "speaking" to those needing a cup of cold water in Jesus' name?

What does your home say to the person who never gets inside the front door? What message does it transmit to someone walking through its halls and rooms for the first time? What effect does it have on those who spend some time there in more intimate and personal relationships?

In offering this idea of silent witness, I don't envision "praying hands" or Christian magazines on the coffee tables. How you use your home and what people sense when they are in it are far more revealing.

As Mr. Samuel implied, quality can be added to this witness through design. Design is more of a continuum rather than a onetime action. It's the process of putting together unrelated things—juxtaposing even the valuable and the trivial if you desire—to develop the "words" that we want our homes to use. It's a way of thinking that will bring the Master's touch and life to otherwise inanimate surroundings. It's having our homes reflect what we really are.

God has ordained good works for you and your family, and verbal expressions of encouragement, support, and the message of salvation will necessarily be a part of their achievement. "For we are God's masterpiece. He has created us anew in Christ Jesus, so that we can do the good things he planned for us long ago" (Ephesians 2:10).

But as it was in Jesus' day, there must be the confirming testimony of two or three witnesses to validate any truth. Realistically, we are nothing more in public than we are in secret, no matter what words we employ. If the silent witness of our homes—this is the *life* that we mentioned at the outset—is inconsistent with our verbal expressions, the effect of our influence for good is blunted.

Won't you join me in exploring these concepts through a "day's journey" into our home? It will be one of many sights and sounds, and you won't likely catch them all at once. The

sights—the aesthetical determinations and decisions embodied in the home's design—are somewhat subjective, revealing how *our* home is, not how yours has to be. The sounds? They're those words of silent witness that can only be fully imparted through the work of the Holy Spirit as he interprets the sights.

Sometimes the words will represent feelings. But other words will go far beyond—even to the character of the occupants. Feelings may come and go, but character endures. Our goal will be to see the character of Christ as manifested in many ways in the home.

Of course, we'll look at practical how-tos, such as furniture placement, the use of color and lighting, and many more. But as important as these are, they are just tools, tools for developing your home into a silent but persuasive witness of God's work in your life.

Having made these promises, let me clarify one thing. My wife, Annabelle, is a private person, and our home is her sanctuary, the very work of her hands. There have been no tours or magazine spreads or commercialization of any sort. But if we can momentarily slip behind the scenes a bit to affirm you and your desires for your home, then we are eager to do that. If we can help you establish a vision, not only for the aesthetical details but also in the way your home's silent witness can be enhanced and revealed, then we will have made some major strides. That's really the only reason this book has been written.

2

Your Home's First Words

TWO WORDS

IT ONLY SEEMS LIKE YESTERDAY
A PAIR OF WORDS CAST US AWAY
FROM SHORES THAT SEEMED SO
SAFE AND FREE FROM PAIN.

AND IN EXCURSIONS HERE AND THERE
WE'VE BUILT SOME CASTLES IN THE AIR
AND REAPED REGRET FOR
LABORS SOWN IN VAIN.

THE DREAMS WE'VE HAD
SOMETIMES TURNED 'ROUND
WHEN WINDS OF CHANGE BLEW US AGROUND
THAT WE MIGHT LEARN HOW
GOD WORKS ALL FOR GOOD.

'TWAS THEN IT SEEMED WE HAD TO LEARN
TO TRIM OUR SAILS AND MAKE THE TURNS
TO BE THE MATES AND
FRIENDS WE KNEW WE SHOULD.

BUT STILL WITH EVERY PASSING YEAR
THE BONDS OF LOVE FROM JOYS AND TEARS
SUSTAIN US WHEN WE'RE
BUFFETED WITH FORCE.

AND THOUGH WE'VE GOT SOME MILES TO GO,
THE WORDS "I DO" SAID LONG AGO
STILL BIND OUR HEARTS AND
KEEP US ON OUR COURSE.[2]

Just how important are first words? So much so that parents' memories and baby books are indelibly imprinted with those first words of their children. "I do," the first words in a new marriage, launch a lifetime of commitment that must surely endure countless struggles. "In the beginning" sets the tone of the entire Bible.

Is it wrong to expect that the "first words" that our homes speak are equally significant? Taking that as a given, just how do our homes speak? And what do they say?

We've already mentioned four words—FAITH, CONTENTMENT, BOLDNESS, and SINCERITY—that are foundational, permeating all else. They are like gentle background music that sets an atmosphere without being obvious or obtrusive. Though they are indistinguishable alone, you'll immediately notice their absence.

[2]"Two Words" © 1997 James McAlister. Written in honor of James and Mary McAlister on their thirtieth wedding anniversary. Used by permission.

But now we want to shift our focus a bit to those words that will be a bit more defined. You may hear them individually as the first words that are clearly distinguishable, though they must still blend with the whole.

Regrettably, first words too often just seem to tumble out of our mouths, creating colorfast impressions that we may later wish were different. But that need not be the case with our homes, where the first word can be preprogrammed with a bit of forethought. And it should undoubtedly be ANTICIPATION!

ANTICIPATION is woven into the fabric of joyous lives with an endless thread of expectations: marriages, births, anniversaries, holidays, the return of Christ, and many others. We all feel a certain sense of ANTICIPATION at the hint of a secret, especially one waiting to be discovered . . . perhaps by us.

Just as the enticement of the unknown has motivated extensive human exploits, such as the search for the *Titanic,* there should be a more subtle (but still compelling) element of mystery in our homes. We don't want something dark and sinister; we want points of acute interest just beyond the grasp of the casual observer that will stir up ANTICIPATION for what's to come, both in the home's design and its message.

The Bible is full of such mysteries. While a brisk reading is commendable, the person who digs a bit can unearth personal nuggets that may solve a problem or open new avenues of understanding. If we approach the Scriptures ANTICIPATING a trove, we are much more likely to walk away satisfied.

ANTICIPATION

The eager expectation that God's promises are true and that he will work through my circumstances to fulfill them

This book will pose some parallels. For browsers, the photographs themselves are an overview, a cornucopia with plenty of juicy tidbits just for the taking. But there is more . . . the stories . . . the secrets . . . the words of silent witness . . . begging for disclosure and discovery.

Hopefully, one enlightenment will lead to another, gradually revealing who we are and what we're about in a way that can provide help and healing to those who have the same goals. Isn't this what ANTICIPATION is all about—not knowing the precise details, but looking forward to what comes next?

I sometimes indulge in a secret pleasure: watching those who pass our home without their being able to see me. Many will slow

THE OAK

This mighty oak, the first thing that is seen as the home is approached, effectively masks the house itself while giving just a hint of what lies beyond. More than "just a tree," it is an astounding 230 years old. Its presence was, in fact, the reason that this building site was chosen.

The benefits of its strength and shade to past generations can only be imagined. But it more than adequately points to the refreshment and retreat—both spiritual and physical—that should characterize a home under God and that others should anticipate. Annabelle and grandsons Calvin and Kent often seek refuge in its shade.

FRONT WALK

There are no steps between the street and the front door, a subtle but inviting welcome to the elderly or infirm. The ramp, meticulously built of Spanish mahogany by a friend and craftsman, alleviates the annoyance of water accumulations at the curb while providing a seamless transition between street and walk. And the swinging gates to the wide, uncluttered walk are always open. Rather than be distracted by external obstacles, we want all our guests to sense concern for their needs.

The house itself is purposely baffled by trees. Incongruous as they may seem, the intentional attempt to meld an airy openness with personal privacy has ANTICIPATION *as its goal.*

down for a closer look, captivated by something. I like to think that what they have seen has incited ANTICIPATION about what else may be just around the bend!

Here's one example. The most prominent feature on our landscape is a huge oak tree in the front yard. More than two hundred years old, it exemplifies the timeless heritage of refuge and strength suggested by such mighty oaks.

We acknowledge, of course, that God is our ultimate refuge and strength and that our trust and confidence must be in him. Still, we want the very sight of this magnificent tree to cause others to anticipate that from the home in its shadow might come "trees of righteousness" who will be rebuilders where devastation and desolation have brought ruin to lives.

> To appoint unto them that mourn in Zion, to give unto them beauty for ashes, the oil of joy for mourning, the garment of praise for the spirit of heaviness; that they might be called trees of righteousness, the planting of the LORD, that he might be glorified. And they shall build the old wastes, they shall raise up the former desolations, and they shall repair the waste cities, the desolations of many generations. (Isaiah 61:3-4, KJV)

Smaller trees baffle the house, providing just a glimpse—a hint, if you will—of what lies beyond. This is the essence of ANTICIPATION, for not even best friends—or God himself, for that matter—tell everything about themselves in a single sitting. Part of the beauty of building relationships is the discreet process of mutual revelation and discovery that underpins ANTICIPATION. It's a step beyond asking, "How are you?" and hoping there won't be an answer!

But such questions must be asked—sometimes without words—if SINCERITY is to be discerned. And if we sincerely ask, our friends will hear something: the intimate appeal of CONCERN.

SECONDARY ENTRANCE

This secondary entrance is actually preferred by some. Rather than have it play second fiddle, it has its own distinctive flavor. The bloom-festooned arbor covered with New Dawn roses partially veils the doorway, and New York bluestone stepping-stones provide easy access.

Why invest so much effort in flowers that only bloom once a year? ANTICIPATION! We look forward to their wonderful blooms each year.

CONCERN goes beyond feeling; it's a quality that springs from the recognition that others have worth. That makes us focus on them, not ourselves. The hearts that hear CONCERN will recognize it . . . even if we never say a word.

But how can others sense something so seemingly intangible if we don't verbalize it? Here's one example: Our home has no steps between the street and the front door, and the walkway is wide and smooth. Can you see how an infirm guest might take notice and anticipate a visit? This inherent CONCERN for their special needs will have an influence.

CONCERN

Displaying sincere attention to the needs of others

We also have a fence, and it has gates at the front walk. In stark contrast to those in many of today's walled subdivisions, though, the low fence has a comely shape, and the gates are always open. Can the lonely anticipate warmth and openness, even from the street? Yes, I think so. On the other hand, barriers designed to hold others away make CONCERN hard to feel.

But the feelings and words our homes exude should not end at the street. Let me illustrate.

Jesus said that we should keep his commandments. While we should certainly endeavor to obey them, that's not the primary meaning of this passage. We are to keep them in front of us, reminders not only of his expectations but also of his promises. "He that hath my commandments, and keepeth them, he it is that loveth me: and he that loveth me shall be loved of my Father, and I will love him, and will manifest myself to him" (John 14:21, KJV).

On the outside jamb of our front door is an ornament—a mezuzah—offered to us by a dear Jewish client. Assuaging his fears of offending us, we eagerly accepted it . . . and have used it with honor. You may recall that a mezuzah is the tiny box that Jews put on their doorposts. Inside the box are some excerpts from their law on a parchment scroll that remind them of the place of God in their lives and the importance of their service to him.

What ANTICIPATION this builds in Jewish visitors! With others it frequently invites conversation and the opportunity to verbally share its silent message of REVERENCE.

FRONT DOOR

Light from the inside radiates a warm, inviting feeling. Whenever the front door is opened, visitors can immediately see through the house "shotgun style" to the gardens in the back! Slivers of both Welcome Room and Daily Room are visible; ANTICIPATION is speaking a little louder.

As with other words of silent witness, REVERENCE must be seen as part of a whole that's held in balance. While we certainly want to set that tone at the outset without running roughshod over anyone, we do have a rich spiritual heritage that doesn't cause us any shame.

Consequently, the front door and its immediate environs are welcoming, inviting, and friendly. The ornament is unobtrusive; you might not even see it.

Past construction decisions notwithstanding, avoid a windowless entrance if you can. Natural light has a way of radiating attractive warmth and welcome—even ANTICIPATION—both inside and out. Other entrances that are regularly used should get similar attention.

For practicality, by the way, I'll be introducing our home room by room, because that's the way a visitor would experience it. Nevertheless, particular words of silent witness will repeatedly echo throughout.

Do you get the idea? A home may have many words of witness, but there should be no disharmony. REVERENCE, CONCERN, SINCERITY, FAITH, and many others must be intertwined, hopefully in seamless unity like the words of a hymn.

REVERENCE

Acknowledgment that God is always at work to mold me into the image of Christ

MEZUZAH

A mezuzah is the tiny box that the Jews put on their doorposts. The excerpts from their law on a parchment scroll remind them of the place of God in their lives and the importance of their service to him.

Hear, O Israel: The LORD our God is one LORD: And thou shalt love the LORD thy God with all thine heart, and with all thy soul, and with all thy might. And these words, which I command thee this day, shall be in thine heart: And thou shalt teach them diligently unto thy children, and shalt talk of them when thou sittest in thine house, and when thou walkest by the way, and when thou liest down, and when thou risest up. And thou shalt bind them for a sign upon thine hand, and they shall be as frontlets between thine eyes. And thou shalt write them upon the posts of thy house, and on thy gates. (Deuteronomy 6:4-9, KJV)

Invisibly woven into the fabric of every room, these words should produce an enchanting, unforgettable melody that draws others into the help and hope that you ultimately want to provide.

The Welcome Room

CHAPTER 3

THE BLOOMING ROSE

GOD'S BEEN GROWING SOMETHING THAT'S
SO ELEGANT AND GRAND,
NURTURED EVER CAREFULLY
WITH GENTLE, LOVING HANDS.

WATERED, PRUNED, AND SLOWLY TRAINED,
IN SPLENDOR SHE DISPLAYS
THE NATURE OF THE ONE ABOVE
WHO'S GROOMED HER FOR THIS DAY.

NOW HER LIFE'S AROMA CLAIMS
AN EVER-WIDENING SPHERE,
INNER BEAUTY MIRRORING
THE ONES WHO'VE HELD HER DEAR.

GIRLHOOD'S JOURNEY'S THUS COMPLETE:
A BUD BECOMES A ROSE,
BLOOMING WITH THE CHARACTER
THAT ONLY GOD BESTOWS.[3]

When you go into someone's home, what immediately makes you feel welcome? I'm probably like most people; I respond to ENTHUSIASM!

A warm, enthusiastic greeting from the hosts at the door immediately puts me at ease, and I can feel at home even among strangers.

But can our mere physical surroundings silently express ENTHUSIASM? I think so, because we can see it so clearly in creation. To me, wildflowers—in an almost endless array of colors, shapes, and sizes—must be the ultimate manifestation of God's enthusiasm for the world that he made. In time, buds explode into full bloom as delicate inner beauty reaches out in fuller expression.

So it is with the ENTHUSIASM of our homes. What we feel on the inside finds an outward display in our surroundings that is contagious.

[3]Excerpt from "The Blooming Rose," written in honor of Rachel Riggan on her sixteenth birthday © 1997 James McAlister. Used by permission.

The opulent glory of King Solomon is legendary, but it could not compare to that of the simple flowers of the field. "And why worry about your clothes? Look at the lilies and how they grow. They don't work or make their clothing, yet Solomon in all his glory was not dressed as beautifully as they are" (Matthew 6:28-29).

When our front door is opened, one of Annabelle's spectacular floral arrangements is the first thing that visitors—even those who don't come inside—see. And when they see the flowers, they feel what we want them to: our ENTHUSIASM that they are there! Flowers and green plants simply mirror our

ENTHUSIASM

The outward expression of the joy that is in my heart

FRONT DOOR

Note the contrasting and varied colors and patterns in the floor, the rug, the wall coverings, the ceiling, and the floral arrangement. Such compilations can be delightfully pleasing to the eye, much more personable that having everything match. Seeing such groupings should raise ANTICIPATION that the rest of the house is just as interesting.

The first goal in analyzing any room should be to determine its color theme. Can you discern the color theme of this room?

It's important to leave a room remembering its basic coloration. That's not to say that all blues need to be a perfect match or that all corals cannot be variants of pinks, melons, or even reds. By association, different blues, greens, and other colors take on a harmonious sameness when put together with a relaxed authority.

Before going into your Welcome Room, try to determine what color is the visual unifying "ribbon." If you're not sure, look at the walls, flooring, ceiling, and fabrics to get a clearer picture.

If necessary, ask yourself, "What impact would walls of [choose a color] or a ceiling of [choose another color] have?" Would color applied to either surface give it a clearer definition?

NOBLE HOUSE

CONSOLE, PICTURES, AND ROCK

The eighteenth-century American console in the Welcome Room groans from the weight of various sizes and styles of picture frames filled with the most current blowups of grandsons Calvin Wesley and Kent Edward, daughter Kirsten, son Kristian, and daughter Katrina and her husband, Tom. The frames—ranging from brass to silver to pewter to no frame at all—form a backdrop that accentuates the rock and amplifies a family's need for God's grace.

Though only partially visible here, Annabelle's magnificent floral arrangement has colors that seem to leap off the page to welcome visitors. Throughout our home, and houses that I work on, lighting can make or break any intended effect. In this instance, there is a very tiny Italian spotlight in the ceiling directly over the arrangement that produces the brilliant radiance. Without it the coloration disappears.

You may have noticed how wonderful diamonds or other gemstones look in the jewelry store, but at home they just don't seem to have the same brilliant sparkle. The difference is the lighting.

---

hearts, and you will find them proclaiming ENTHUSIASM from almost every room.

I hope that you've been anticipating something: discovering the story behind the unusual name of this chapter! Just beyond the front door is what most people unimaginatively call an entrance or foyer. We've jettisoned these time-worn monikers in favor of Welcome Room. What a pleasant foreshadowing—a hint of many a welcome to come—in just a name! After all, the idea of welcome is not confined to a single location . . . or a room . . . or even a Welcome Room. But our homes must express it clearly throughout with many words of silent witness.

When Jesus said, "Come to Me, all who are weary and heavy-laden" (Matthew 11:28, NASB), it was his way of extending a welcome at the front door, so to speak. But he couldn't stop there, for weary souls are not satisfied with hollow entreaty. His promise of rest is the kind of substantive encouragement that we all need.

MIRROR AND LIGHTING

Every possible kind of lighting application has been included in the Welcome Room:

- *A hanging glass bell lantern*
- *Italian accent lighting and wall washers, all installed in the ceiling*
- *Wall-hung sconces*
- *Soft, silk-shaded table lighting*

As with the tall clock, verticality is emphasized by the mirror. Though this room is spacious enough, mirrors tend to open up rooms that may be a bit confining.

The discovery of our precious grandson Calvin's autism ushered in one of the darkest moments of our lives. Not content to let us be discouraged, our pastor and his wife brought us a gift. In one sense, it's only an ordinary rock. But the word *grace* carved on one side is more than a subtle reminder to "insiders" that God's grace is sufficient in even the most stressful, difficult times.

ENDURANCE

Withstanding life's trials until God's work has been accomplished

Paul found it so when he wrote, "He said unto me, My grace is sufficient for thee: for my strength is made perfect in weakness. Most gladly therefore will I rather glory in my infirmities, that the power of Christ may rest upon me" (2 Corinthians 12:9, KJV).

Just as Jesus said that the stones will cry out, our rock cries, "ENDURANCE."

The rock has encouraged us to endure and "stay in the fight" to see the work of God accomplished, not only in our lives but also in Calvin's.

Clare Cooper Marcus, professor of architecture at the University of California-Berkeley, says that people relate to their homes with as much intensity as they do to other people, especially during times of crisis. Our rock is a perfect example.

To those who may not know its story, it catalyzes ENDURANCE in a way with potent precedence and significance. When the Israelites were about to enter the Promised Land, they built an altar with stones taken from the then-parted Jordan River. Why? To establish common ground with those who had not experienced God's deliverance in travail when they asked, "What do these stones

TALL CLOCK

The clock has an interesting background. According to the provenance written inside the door, it was made between 1710 and 1730. It was in terrible shape when I found it, but we love it because it's a picture of "beauty from ashes." Plus, innards of brass silently tell something about the English farmer who made it: ENDURANCE to build something that endures the test of time. Isn't that what we all want?

Vertical elements such as stripes can be used to "push" the ceiling upward to give a more stately feel. Plus, verticality is emphasized even more by the clock. Note that a number of stripes occur in this space:

- *Striped wall covering*
- *Tone-on-tone striped fabric on the settee*
- *A horizontally placed lineal border at the ceiling and baseboard*

mean?" Do you see the connection? The rocks literally "cried out" for expression and explanation, and objects of particular import in your home can as well.

> We will use these stones to build a memorial. In the future, your children will ask, "What do these stones mean to you?" Then you can tell them, "They remind us that the Jordan River stopped flowing when the Ark of the Lord's covenant went across." These stones will stand as a permanent memorial among the people of Israel. (Joshua 4:6-7)

ANTIQUE CLOCK

A detail showing the handwritten provenance authenticating the age of the tall clock in the Welcome Room to be as early as 1710.

Giving such an object a place of honor—right there with a host of family pictures in our Welcome Room—opens many doors. Prominence, particularly when something as mundane as a rock is involved, implies a value that others can't help but notice and will often question. The words of silent witness can then seek their own course.

Though we'll see more of it as we go, the discovery of the story behind an object such as the rock reinforces ANTICIPATION in ways that would no more yield to planning than the stories themselves. Do you have such objects? They can probably speak more clearly than any clever story.

Without preaching, family pictures say, "Pull together; a family lives here. We care about each other, and we care about you." Through a powerful medium that we'll visit again, they substantiate the quality of LOYALTY . . . LOYALTY within a real family in a day when families are so fragmented. And they say it so subtly to those who may feel the need for family or for close relationships.

Every family has struggles, ours included. But when visitors hear ENDURANCE and LOYALTY in unison, we want them to realize that with God's help, problems can be worked out.

Will this happen accidentally? By no means! In the first chapter, I alluded to the part that interior design can play and promised to offer some practical suggestions. Design is much like the frame on a painting: it should enhance and embellish but not overshadow. If proper design technique can be engaged to bring the words of silent witness unobtrusively to the forefront, so much the better.

To illustrate, I just mentioned the family unity and loyalty that's implied by pictures. But how can unity and loyalty in relationships be reinforced through design?

LOYALTY

Maintaining faithfulness to God and others, even during trying times

Designwise, color is probably the greatest unifier in a room. The effective application of a *particular* color can do more to cause a room to be cohesively successful than any amount of carefully selected (or even costly) objects. In essence, therefore, the message of the room harmonizes with that of the pictures.

Here's one approach. Once you have determined the thread of color that runs throughout the furnishings of a room, you may want to use it on the walls or ceiling to pull things together. Ceilings, by the way, are usually the most neglected surface in a room, but you can use color and patterns there as well.

God made all colors to be used, but some can certainly be spiritless. So if you need an inspirational jump start, return to historical design, particularly eighteenth-century combinations and applications. On the other hand, more contemporary combinations—such as rooms painted in combinations of lavender and greens—need not be out of line. Winterthur, the DuPont residence (now a museum) in Wilmington, Delaware, is an example of the exceptional application of eighteenth-century color and design that can be applied to today's homes.

When I mention historical design, I'm thinking of something that's "correct," some-

WELCOME ROOM—BACKWARD GLANCE

In all of life, it's helpful to look at situations from different angles. Here we have a backward view of the Welcome Room, showing how it looks to those who are leaving the house. Chairs in the room provide a homey, welcoming functionality. Rich lighting along with more pictures and plants that are only seen from this direction say that though a visit may have ended, the welcome has not.

thing that's been done with a great deal of knowledge, thought, and attention to detail. This is evident when comparing French Louis XVI with English Adam–detailed design. Both have lineal qualities—such as fluted legs and details—that are very similar.

The more exciting thing about period design, however, is how skillfully and ambitiously color was applied to walls, moldings, and ceilings. Startling color applications are used to define door moldings from walls, and doors from door moldings. In one striking example of English design—the Royal Pavilion completed in 1823 by King George IV in Brighton, England—literally every surface has some applied decoration. In some cases inset panels have been upholstered with dramatically colored embroidered fabrics, tapestries, and even tone-on-tone silk damask wall upholsteries.

Ceilings have extremely ambitious trellis patterns—some directly attributable to Thomas Chippendale. Colors used throughout are aggressive combinations of the strongest emerald greens, cerulean blues stronger than any Pacific waters imaginable, and golds and yellows close to the color of saffron. Each color is defined with the use of moldings that are basically ivory overlaid with brilliant gold leaf and outlined with the darkest of teal green striping.

Due to the scale of these rooms, colors with such intensity in their combinations "work." In today's environment, judicious doses of the same colorations used more sparingly are still equally effective.

Language is a vehicle that enables words to be melded into a whole that's greater than the sum of its parts. Even common words—Lincoln's Gettysburg Address comes to mind—can inspire, encourage, and motivate when delivered with honest, open sincerity. So it should be with the silent witness of our homes. Thus, even the words we've already encountered—such as ANTICIPATION, ENDURANCE, and LOYALTY—can't really stand alone. They must be harmonized and undergirded by the many others that we will hear.

4

The Daily Room

CHAPTER 4

THOSE HANDS

I FELT THOSE HANDS ON MINE TODAY
AS I TRIED TO FIND A WAY
TO DO A JOB I KNEW NOT HOW TO DO.

THEY GUIDED ME WITH SKILL SO RARE
I KNEW HE MUST HAVE BEEN RIGHT THERE
TO LEAD ME THROUGH THE JOB HE USED TO DO.

WHEN I WAS YOUNG, HE'D OFT COME NEAR—
WITH HANDS ON MINE, A GENTLE STEER—
TO TRACE FOR ME THE STEPS I'D HAVE TO DO.

AND WHEN I SOUGHT THE JOB TO SPEED,
WITH KIND RESTRAINT THOSE HANDS WOULD LEAD
TO BETTER WORK THAN I WAS WONT TO DO.

THOUGH NOW BY DEATH FROM THIS LIFE FREED,
HE LEFT ME WHAT HE KNEW I'D NEED:
MY FATHER'S HANDS STILL SHOW ME WHAT TO DO.[4]

The wife of my coauthor, James, was touched by his account of how he had helped their son, Barrett, learn a new task by physically guiding his hands through the difficult steps. She asked James to write a poem describing the feelings that Barrett might have when, upon being a father himself, he would reflect on how his father had taught him.

In a nutshell, this poem reminds us that though teachable moments are transitory, they should leave an enduring legacy of gentle, persistent instruction. We find this thought in the Bible as well, where effective child training was to be meted out in small chips rather than in large chunks.

[4]"Those Hands" © 1997 James McAlister. Used by permission.

> And you must commit yourselves wholeheartedly to these commands I am giving you today. Repeat them again and again to your children. Talk about them when you are at home and when you are away on a journey, when you are lying down and when you are getting up again. (Deuteronomy 6:6-7)

The same principle applies to other relationships. They are built minute by minute in the seemingly routine activities of daily life. Opportunity doesn't pause for the few "right" times.

I am of Norwegian ancestry, and that culture seems to have a pretty good handle on this concept. In bygone days, Norwegian family life centered in the *dagligstué,* or "daily room." It was much more the hub of activity than its rather limp, westernized "family room" counterpart. It was in the *dagligstué* that families interacted, friends were entertained, relationships were built, memories were forged.

In our home, the Daily Room is the focus from which most activity radiates, and it reflects our attempt to facilitate informal but meaningful interactions in the spirit of the *dagligstué.*

ORDERLINESS

Arranging my surroundings to maximize their usefulness

Order and flexibility cooperatively form the foundation for a successful Daily Room. And believe it or not, these essential qualities are not mutually exclusive.

The best kind of room is one that is not confusing in its layout and is not so precious in its appearance that people don't want to use it. Consequently, order is possibly the most important element of any well-designed room, and our rooms should speak of ORDERLINESS in a user-friendly way.

Though this definition may seem a bit sterile, ORDERLINESS is very practical. It must have been foremost in Noah's mind as he planned how to arrange people, animals, and food for the months on the ark! How else could all have survived?

> "Bring a pair of every kind of animal—a male and a female—into the boat with you to keep them alive during the flood. Pairs of each kind of bird and each kind of animal, large and small alike, will come to you to be kept alive. And remember, take enough food for your family and for all the animals." So Noah did everything exactly as God had commanded him. (Genesis 6:19-22)

DAILY ROOM—OVERVIEW, CABINET CLOSED

The Daily Room has sixteen patterned plaid fabrics in addition to patterns and textures that occur on tables and walls. Even with such variety, "ribbons of colors" provide a subtle cohesiveness that helps justify seemingly unrelated colors or colorations.

*Most good color schemes have as their foundation a rug or are based on fabric, typically called a lead fabric, from which all the other colors in the room emanate. My formula works this way: beginning with a blue/***green** *plaid, next to it a* **green**/**yellow** *plaid, then a* **yellow**/red, *next a* red/*purple, etc.*

As you use colors (blue, for example), pull together everything that's blue, and don't be concerned that the blues don't match perfectly. Rather, think as an artist does: all shades of blue are found in blue. Continually try to avoid predictability and sameness.

DAILY ROOM—OVERVIEW, CABINET OPENED

We have wood flooring throughout the house, and the patterns go in different directions. The Welcome Room even has a herringbone-patterned wood floor to give a bit of interest.

The Daily Room has an oversized stenciled rug that almost looks like sisal. On top of that lies a rug that was made in China and has all the colorations—mostly periwinkle and greens and corals—that Annabelle enjoys.

Remote controls for stereo and TV are contained in a flat, open wicker basket or tray that also holds the day's mail, periodicals, catalogs, etc., awaiting final review before being put away. Annabelle's most current reading can be found in stacks in this room as well as others.

Even a TV (seen on the far side of the room) or a computer can be effectively concealed and blended with a room's decor with proper cabinetry. If not, consider them appliances, being honest about what they are as well as what they're intended for.

Small chairs at the coffee table affirm to children that they are welcome. Without excuse, the coffee table has children's toys on, under, and around it—either just lying there or organized in little boxes and baskets.

Thankfully, our task is not of such grand proportions. Nevertheless, there are similar considerations. When putting together a floor plan, for example, keep it logical by remembering the sizes of your furniture that can only fit into a particular place.

But the effect of ORDERLINESS can't be completely realized without FLEXIBILITY.

Here's one way our Daily Room silently speaks of FLEXIBILITY: seating is in the round to avoid the confinements of the "conversational groupings" that appear decorative but thwart conversation and interaction. We have tried not to artificially force seating patterns, and most people seem to love the arrangement. It goes a long way toward restructuring the circumstances that create the small clumps of people that naturally exclude the more reticent.

FLEXIBILITY

Not being rigid in my approach to achieving my goals

Our grandson Calvin's autism has motivated us to seek an effective blend of both ORDERLINESS and FLEXIBILITY. It has, for example, inspired in us a deliberate attitude of "organized clutter" that relieves a lot of pressure, both for him and for us. Simply put, some toys are just never put away; they are always available to Calvin. In addition, glass doors on the closets in the Daily Room reveal, rather than hide, contents to Calvin in an uncomplicated way.

There are other toys in the house as well, but the Daily Room is Calvin's domain. That's part of the overall design. We want him to be comfortable there. Our house is to be lived in, literally touched and felt until we are a part of it. As a by-product, other children also relish the goodies within their easy reach!

I long for homemakers to understand the importance of not hiding everything. We must get around that if our homes are to be used and useful. Let's be creative about it.

Think about newspapers a moment. They're messy, and the ink can easily soil furniture. We have a rack—the kind of thing that might be seen in libraries or in the dining rooms of

DAILY ROOM—CLOSE-UP OF PICTURES, CABINET, CAMELS

Furnishings that appear to have been gathered over time have a special appeal, especially when they reflect the unique tastes of the owners. The camels—I just love camels—are a case in point.

If you want to give a home instant age and a finished appearance, nothing does it like beautiful wallpapers, whether patterned or strongly textured. To give it a really finished appearance, nothing will do it like your grandsons on their Tiny Tyke tractors barreling through the house!

Toys and photos proclaim life: a home is not for looking but for feeling and touching and hugging. Calvin's Swedish Brio train set is clearly visible here. Original artwork by our son, Kristian, adds a special flavor, as do the varied shapes and sizes of the frames on the pictures.

certain hotels—that the newspaper hangs on. My father-in-law made it for me, and I love it. I don't get newsprint all over the furniture, and the paper is always convenient.

I realize that you may not have the same space that we have in our Daily Room, but I encourage you to work with what you have to keep your room friendly, inviting, and uncomplicated. There still must be a method to the madness, however, to keep disarray from taking over and reigning.

There are no doors between the Daily Room and the other rooms; the room flows into the others. This allows us to interact with each other, which is the way we like to live.

Because of Calvin, we've learned a new word. In one sense, we've always known it, but it's taken on a richer, fuller meaning because of him. To us, it's far more than a word because it underpins so much else. The word is SENSITIVITY. Our homes must say it clearly.

Let me try to explain how SENSITIVITY can affect both ORDERLINESS and FLEXIBILITY.

Before Calvin's birth, we were certainly aware of many of the difficulties faced by special-needs people. My heart always goes out to them because of the trials they face.

But with Calvin's needs, my horizon was immediately and dramatically broadened far beyond my expectations. In short order, I was made aware of just how deeply hurts can go but still not be seen by others. Consequently, I seek to make our home a place where we can "rejoice with them that do rejoice, and weep with them that weep" (Romans 12:15, KJV).

SENSITIVITY

Perceiving the real needs of those with whom I have contact

Many of Calvin's needs are clear-cut; we can easily tell what they are. But that's not always the case. The same thing is true with others, and people will seldom reveal their deepest feelings until mutual trust has long been established.

That's where perception comes in. It goes without saying that we all have needs, spoken or unspoken. If people can sense that we perceive needs that they haven't overtly revealed, then we are in a position of sensitivity and usefulness.

How can a home's design help it to effectively speak about our SENSITIVITY? Part of the answer lies in an understanding of human nature. One hesitancy to opening up

DAILY ROOM—COZY CORNER

I don't believe that there is a room in the house that doesn't have a cozy corner[5]*, a place where Annabelle can quietly go to study the Scripture or where we, with our respective prayer partners, can steal away to confer with or encourage each other.*

A comfortable chair in which to read the newspaper, watch the news, or listen to music is a plus. Make sure there is adequate reading light next to that chair.

The newspaper and rack are simultaneously unobtrusive and accessible.

[5]"Cozy corner" was coined by Edith Dean, coauthor of my first book, *Interior Decorating: A Reflection of the Creator's Design.*

is the desire not to "be a bother" by revealing hurts and needs to someone else. In actuality, we resist putting others in the position of making accommodations and adjustments for us.

But if some of those adjustments have already been made, we're already on the right track. Remember the seating? By not forcing Miss Shy to converse with Mr. Forceful, we may open some doors of ministry.

Our Daily Room has more that twenty separate fabric patterns, the bulk of them being varied plaids, even though "ribbons of color" provide a feeling of continuity. In a very subtle sense, this says that our tastes don't rigidly conform to a particular style—either in furnishings or in people.

I coined the term "ribbons of color" to both describe and validate the assemblage of numerous but seemingly unrelated patterns and colorations in one space or room.

Let's say you have a fabric or a rug with varied colors. I call this the "lead" fabric. If it has blues, violets, greens, reds, or yellows, you can then use almost any of these colors throughout the room. An all green sofa, for example, could have pillows that have not only green but also any of the aforementioned colors. An adjacent chair would typically have the color of either the sofa or the pillows.

Start with a lively patterned fabric, and let one of its colors translate to a single color in the next piece. These colors—whether they are blue, violet, red, gold, or green—essentially "move" into the adjoining piece of furniture. But you are not just limited to a single color in this transition; you may use any combinations of these same colors.

This is similar to the way needlepoints are woven. Some of the colors recur frequently; others appear quite infrequently. But the concept gives us the freedom from obsessing that everything must match absolutely perfectly.

If you look at a red apple painted by one of the great masters, you will see that it's really made up of violets, greens, oranges, and possibly blues. Yet the finished product emulates a red apple, which the eye accepts. The same is true of a real flower.

Rooms should thus be designed or colored in a "painterly" manner. As long as you pull some common color from one piece of furniture to the next, you have a ribbon of color that gently binds the separated pieces

WELCOME ROOM—BACKWARD GLANCE

A successful room will have warmth and comfort coupled with logic and substance with careful attention to proportion. The feel is also important. Is it cool, hot, clean, stuffy?

Notice how even unpredictably varied patterns and textures give an inviting appearance. While I'm not a proponent of sameness of color throughout a house, notice how the Daily Room and the Welcome Room play off each other using different doses of similar colors. This eliminates a jolt to the senses as one moves from one space to another.

WELCOME ROOM—DRAWINGS OF FURNITURE-PLACEMENT OPTIONS

Numerous furniture-placement options provide both ORDERLINESS *and* FLEXIBILITY. *Most furniture has purposely been kept away from the fireplace. It's used only a small part of the year, and this keeps it from being overemphasized.*

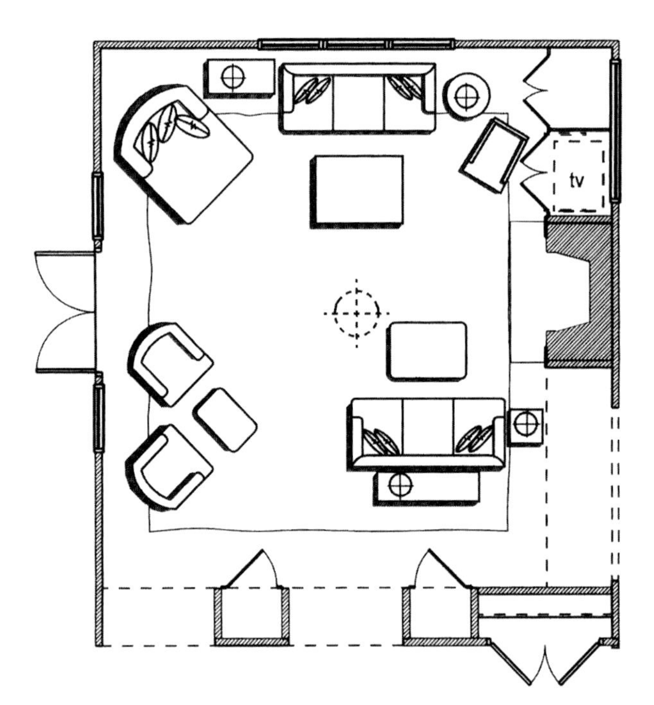

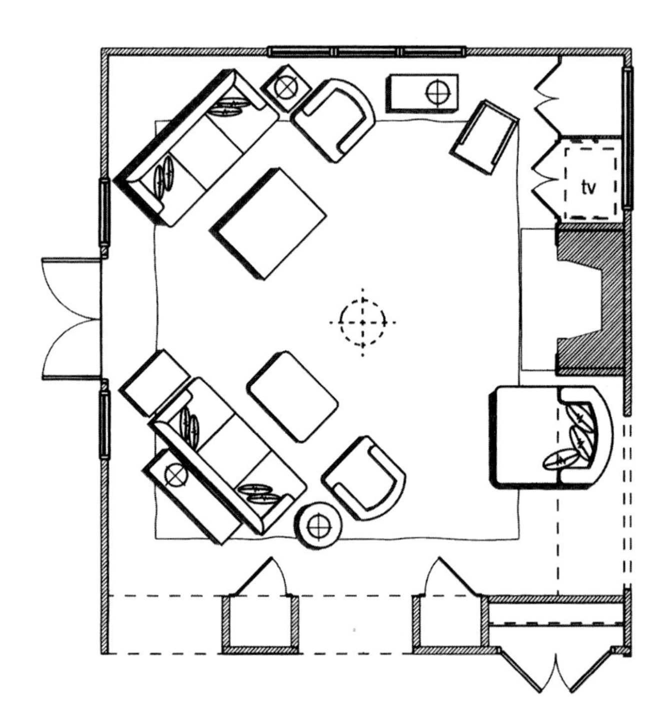

PLAN A

This is the plan as it appears in the photos. The two sofas anchor the room and can accommodate ten to twelve people for seating in the round. If necessary, each can be used independently for smaller seating requirements.

PLAN B

Here both sofas have been angled to create a different kind of balance as they face more toward the fireplace and the entertainment center. Note how the oversized chaise has been positioned to the right of the fireplace, allowing someone to lie on it and snuggle close to the fire.

into a composite that the eye quickly embraces. You thus establish a relationship among seemingly unrelated colors because there is a subtle common denominator in moving from piece to piece. This gives a more natural feel that takes some of the artificial "sting" out of a design that might otherwise appear forced or contrived.

If we can feel the hurts of others and tear down natural barriers to their hearts by the way we arrange our homes, they will sense our concern without our having to say a thing. Having accomplished this, perhaps we can "put our hands on theirs" as in the poem . . . and help them through the difficulty. That's SENSITIVITY in action.

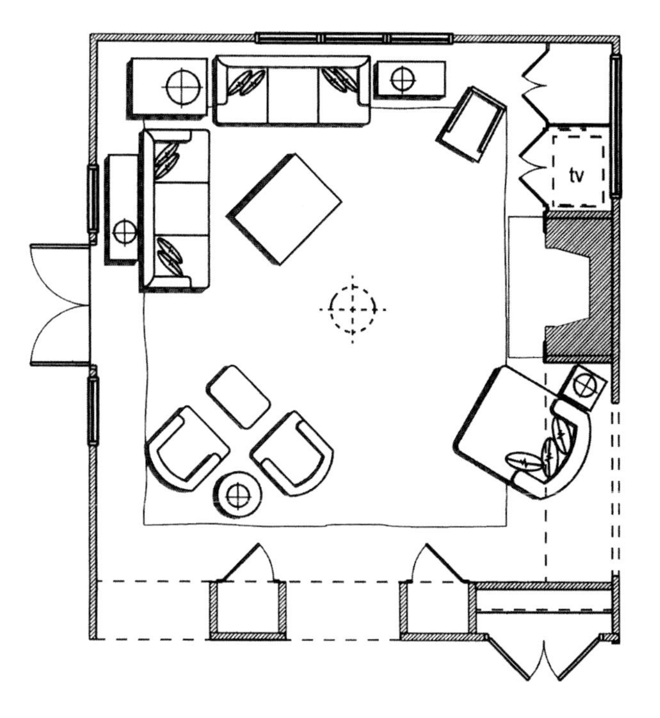

PLAN C

This is the more conventional arrangement for the two sofas. The disadvantage of their being at right angles to each other is one of foot space. On occasion, feet can collide.

The Living Room

CHAPTER 5

MIGHTY WARRIORS

MIGHTY WARRIORS, GLEAMING WHITE,
STANDING READY, DAY AND NIGHT.
FULL OF POWER, GOD'S OWN HOST,
GUARDING WHAT HE LOVES THE MOST.

UNSEEN DANGERS, HERE AND THERE,
YET THEY TRIP THE FOWLER'S SNARE.
SATAN'S ARMIES, BENT ON HARM,
THEY CAN STOP WITHOUT ALARM.

NEVER LAUGHING, NEVER WEEP,
NEVER SLUMBER, NEVER SLEEP.
NOT CONSTRAINED BY TIME OR SPACE,
THEY BEHOLD THE FATHER'S FACE.

ALWAYS READY TO OBEY
HIS COMMANDS WITHOUT DELAY.
EVER WATCHFUL, WITHOUT FEAR;
CHILDREN'S ANGELS, ALWAYS NEAR.[6]

Why do parents seem to readily embrace the concept of guardian angels for their children? Perhaps because they acknowledge their own limitations and abilities to protect their little ones from countless dangers, many of which they can't even see. On the other hand, angels, who transcend the tangible and operate in realms where our senses and capabilities can't take us, are better suited to the task.

But are there guardian angels? Apparently so, based on the high authority of Jesus' words: "Beware that you don't despise a single one of these little ones. For I tell you that in heaven their angels are always in the presence of my heavenly Father" (Matthew 18:10).

[6]"Mighty Warriors" © 1997 James McAlister. Used by permission.

Normally hidden to the eye, these agents of God stand ever ready to act at his behest. They provide but one example where the unseen is more real and more powerful than the seen.

The apostle Paul knew this well, and his focus on the unseen helped him endure affliction and trial:

> Our light affliction, which is but for a moment, worketh for us a far more exceeding and eternal weight of glory; While we look not at the things which are seen, but at the things which are not seen: for the things which are seen are temporal; but the things which are not seen are eternal. (2 Corinthians 4:17-18, KJV)

The same idea is woven into the fabric of commonsense wisdom. "Beauty is only skin deep" and "You can't judge a book by its cover" both emphasize that what's below the surface has the greater significance.

CALVIN AND ANGELS

Grandsons Calvin Wesley and Kent Edward are first in our hearts, and reminders of them are found throughout the house.

This picture of Calvin—taken two weeks before we knew of his autism—reminds us of how powerless we felt when we were told. Shortly after, these angels were given to us by a family that was unaware of our struggles. But what encouragement the angels brought!

It is so comforting to realize that angels, those invisible agents of God, are ever at work to carry out his bidding in protecting our grandsons. We are always eager to share the story—as unseen as guardian angels themselves—of our GRATEFULNESS to God and our friends behind these seemingly ordinary Christmas figures that are always on display.

Can we make some reasonable application of this concept to the home? Can the unseen really be more important than the seen?

Think a moment about your acquaintances. There are probably some with whom you have a most cordial relationship that is, by all outward appearances, quite successful. But perhaps you sense that there is something missing, an unseen spark that comes from the heart-to-heart connection that takes relationships to a deeper level. Even marriages languish without it.

Here's how it can work. On the surface an object is no more than what it appears to be. A shoe is a shoe is a shoe, so to speak, and can be the basis of a sterile discussion on shoes.

But if the shoe is an old baby shoe, its leather and stitching are but shadows—shadows of victories and defeats, tragedies and triumphs, struggles for maturity and independence—of a departed childhood. Parents understand, and stories that bind relationships can be shared. I've seen lockets, pictures, and even snippets of hair unexpectedly become catalysts for discussion times that drew people together with memories of home. A sentimental object can have great power for nurturing a warm, companionable atmosphere in a home.

Some might dismiss this as unnecessary sentimentality, but I don't see it that way. To me, real living begins when meaningful relationships develop. And could there be a better vehicle than a "Living" Room, where seemingly ordinary objects might envelop stories that will forge lifelong bonds?

GRATEFULNESS

A thankful response to the benefits that have come into my life

There might be many words of silent witness behind any object, and I'll mention a practical trilogy in a moment. But first, let me mention one that is rooted with deep feelings, feelings of GRATEFULNESS for a priceless friendship bound up in an object worth only ten cents.

Several years ago one of my friends, a service-station owner, suffered a serious heart attack. When I went to visit him in the hospital, I learned that he might have to have a leg amputated due to circulation complications.

Two days before the surgery, my friend called me collect from his hospital room to wish me a happy birthday.

LIVING ROOM—SEATING IN THE ROUND

Seating in the round helps break down the constraints of contrived "conversational groupings" that seem to be in vogue. This room echoes that theme so that everyone should be able to participate, whether they are there for a meeting or just for conversation.

Numerous illustrations of RESOURCEFULNESS *are tucked away in the Living Room. Notice how the curtains in the center of the far wall are pulled back on just the right side. The fabric is from the curtains in our last house, but there wasn't enough for the longer curtains in this house. A bit of* CREATIVITY *produced this scheme, which has worked out well both aesthetically and economically. Though you can't see it, the seam (where the fabric from a "sacrificial" pair of curtains was added) has been made where the curtains are tied back to the wall.*

The two rugs—of identical patterns and colors—were in separate rooms in our previous home. Annabelle really liked their colorations and design, so we found a way to use them together rather than buying a new rug for that space.

RESOURCEFULNESS

Making the most of the resources available to me

Visiting him after the surgery, I thanked him for his thoughtfulness in spite of his own serious afflictions. Until I mentioned the call, he didn't even remember it. Once reminded, however, he remembered some of the details, particularly that he had called collect. Not one to be indebted, he insisted that I take the dime he offered to pay for the call.

I've tried to learn to lay aside pride and graciously receive whatever people want to give, but this was hard. I was touched by his offer, however, and took the dime and put it in a small display case in our Living Room.

Sometime later, my friend and his brother came to our home, where he recounted both the call and how it had initially escaped his memory. I mentioned his repayment, retrieved the case, and showed them the dime. Tears of GRATEFULNESS flowed freely from his eyes as that small object—itself of little value—

ENGLISH FARM HUTCH

The previous picture shows the Living Room as it appeared for the first two years. This more recent picture illustrates how the placement of a single piece of furniture (such as this Queen Anne English farm hutch) can markedly alter the look and feel of a room.

We fell in love with this nineteenth-century English farm hutch the first time we saw it, but the decision to bring it home required quite a bit of deliberation. We finally determined that it would be perfect to hold the porcelains that Annabelle has acquired over many years. Though you can't tell from this picture, they are an assortment of heirlooms, antiques, and brand-new purchases.

The hutch and the mixed-and-matched porcelains inject a bit of rural flavor, toning down the formal edge that our Living Room had. The hutch has also forced us to move one sofa slightly forward. This puts people a little closer together and helps conversation flow more freely.

released a flood of feelings from his heart. We really *lived* that day.

Words of silent witness need not be limited to such intimate stories of the heart. These words will no doubt find expression in practical ways that can be of particular encouragement. I alluded to three words of witness that, like good friends, usually run together. They are RESOURCEFULNESS, CREATIVITY, and THRIFTINESS. Let me illustrate how they cooperate with one another.

There's something tantalizing about the curtains in our Living Room that will often elicit comments about their uniqueness. While the finished product is special in its own right, only those who inquire a bit further discover the story behind the curtains.

Annabelle loved the fabric (which had been discontinued) of the curtains in our last house and wanted to bring them with us. Unfortunately, the windows in the new house were markedly taller. Rather than count the cause as lost, we sought to be RESOURCEFUL and preserve what we already had. We concluded that the fabric from one pair would have to be sacrificed to lengthen the others.

Even so, there was a price to pay; we were shy a full pair of curtains! Still, we sought to make do with what we had, so a bit of CREATIVITY resolved the issue in a unique way. The pictures illustrate it far better than I can explain it!

CREATIVITY

Seeing new ways to get around the roadblocks to achievement

While it's certainly possible to have a picture-perfect room assembled totally from new items, I almost always prefer furnishings and accessories with a history. I encourage those with like sentiments to harmoniously blend both CREATIVITY and RESOURCEFULNESS to make use of their treasures. In proper mixture, THRIFTINESS is a natural result.

The issue of how much to spend in a particular situation often arises, and there's really no pat answer. THRIFTINESS is more complex than spending as little as possible. Rather, it has one eye on the long run. It is really "invest-

ENJOYING ROSES
REDOUTÉ'S ROSES

MULTIPLE FLORAL PATTERNS

Seemingly unrelated patterns and things, if put together with an attitude of authority, can result in a unique cohesiveness unattainable with preplanned matches. At least twelve different floral patterns appear here. Such mixtures take the edge off the widespread misconception that everything has to be a perfect match and fit.

The bulldog stool—probably given that name because of the shape of its legs—was handmade by my father. My mother needle-pointed the cover, and it is truly a treasure of the heart. As a child, I would turn it upside down and pretend that it was my ship. Some would say that the stool is underscaled for the room or that it doesn't fit with the other pieces. But design has little or no value unless the heart gains control, regardless of how things seem to fit in a technical sense.

Note the economy of fabric in these curtains; this set has only a left side, which mirrors another set with only a right side in the same room. This is how we compromised to account for the fabric sacrificed to lengthen the other curtains. Rather than being distracting, the effect has proven to be both workable and appealing.

Books on the coffee table are one of the strongest ribbons that bind all of our rooms together.

ment buying," or making purchases that will provide the best use of your money over time. Wall coverings are one example; they generally provide a better long-term economy than does paint even though the initial investment is higher.

If you have a special piece of furniture that you really want to keep, refinishing or recovering worn surfaces can probably be justified on that basis. Otherwise, look at the costs before you decide. Careful shopping with attention to construction and materials can produce some excellent buys, even from discount furniture stores.

THRIFTINESS

Avoiding unnecessary expenditures

In the end, there's something far more significant to others than the spaciousness of your rooms or how much you spent to fill them. These considerations may make an initial impression, but the stories in your objects and furnishings are the words that bring any room to life. They hold the secrets others want to discover and experiences they're eager to share. Like bright arrows, they can pierce a hard outer facade to touch the unseen feelings of the heart.

COFFEE TABLE AND STOOL

This coffee table, custom-made in England to our specifications, has legs patterned after those we had seen on an antique buffet, which we subsequently bought. It can accommodate eight people—some sitting on the floor if they desire—for coffee and dessert.

Note the contrast: The old handmade stool and the new custom-made table. Both have stories . . . very different stories. And stories from both old and new can build bridges to others' needs.

RIBBONS OF BOOKS

Books form strong ribbons, both among rooms and within particular rooms. Notice that the shelves of books are not interrupted with other accessories. Shelves should have one or the other. Otherwise the arrangement is affected and often unworkable.

On the top shelf is an epergne, a crystal bowl on a silver stand, which belonged to my great-grandparents. It is the only thing in the house relegated to an unreachable place.

Though not visible here, this bookcase also contains the small display case with the dime. To the eye, the epergne and the dime form a sharp contrast in material worth. But as treasures of the heart—where valuation is unseen and immeasurable—they stand side by side. They may not match, but they surely fit.

KRISTIAN'S ARTWORK

Son Kristian's artwork is given a place of prominence here. In contrast to other places where we have used plastic frames or no frames at all, worthy frames confirm both the artist and the painting. If a parent so chooses to affirm a child's work, this is one way to do it.

Virtually every surface, ceilings included, has wall coverings. From a design standpoint, they offer almost limitless combinations of colors, textures, and patterns. Very practical, they have a typical life span of ten to twenty years, two to four times that of paint. Though they cost more to install, they provide the better long-term investment.

The Settling Room

6

THAT LITTLE BOY

A GHOST WAS IN THE HALL TODAY;
THAT LITTLE BOY HAD COME TO PLAY.
FOR ONE BRIEF MOMENT, LAUGHTER LONG;
IN JUST ANOTHER HE WAS GONE.
BUT IN THAT FLASH IN MY MIND'S EYE,
I SAW SO MUCH OF DAYS GONE BY.

BUT NOW THOSE TIMES, THOSE PRECIOUS YEARS,
HAVE SLIPPED AWAY DESPITE MY FEARS.
SPENT DAY BY DAY, THEY SEEMED TO LAST,
BUT LOOKING BACK, TOO QUICKLY PASSED.
IT'S ALL DONE NOW, MY CHANCE IS GONE
TO SHAPE A SOUL AND SPIRIT STRONG.

OUR TIME'S SO SHORT, LET'S NOT FORGET
TO LIVE EACH DAY WITHOUT REGRET.
LET'S GIVE OUR ALL, SO LOOKING BACK,
WE'LL FEEL NO SHAME, NOR LOSS, NOR LACK,
ON HAVING WASTED YEARS, ILL SPENT,
AND LEFT A CHILD WITHOUT GOD'S BENT.[7]

For most of us, hope springs from tomorrow, when anything is possible. On the other hand, today is usually relegated to the routine chores that somehow seem to always interfere with tomorrow. But today can slip away almost unnoticed, taking with it the opportunities that it brought.

In a sense, we do acknowledge the importance of the seemingly ordinary trifles of today, but we seldom comprehend their full import until they are seen from the vantage point of tomorrow. If a day brings conflict or struggle, it's important to resolve it before the day ends. "'Don't sin by letting anger gain control over you.' Don't let the sun go down while you are still angry, for anger gives a mighty foothold to the Devil" (Ephesians 4:26-27).

[7]Excerpt from "That Little Boy" © 1996 James McAlister. Used by permission.

This is so true in family relationships, where small hurts, if left unresolved, can cause a root of bitterness to spring up. If that happens, we may look back and count the wasted days—days that could have been more profitably spent building one another up—through tears of regret.

The home should be the oil that settles the troubled seas of life. While bedrooms naturally evoke an image of settling down for the night, the picture need not—indeed, it should not—end so simply. Our master bedroom has been the place where so many difficult issues of life were brought to resolution. Settled, as it were, in a peaceful, joyous, and harmonious way. That's why we call it the Settling Room.

Our children are grown now, but earlier days would often find all five of us on the fifty-four-inch mattress in our bedroom for times of fun and conversation. As the years passed, the children would still come home from their evening activities, pile onto our bed, and share the night's events.

No subject was ever ruled out of bounds; we wanted open communication in neutral territory. Whenever conflicts have come, we've endeavored to settle them with PATIENCE; the passage of time only makes rankled feelings harder to iron out.

Our Settling Room speaks of PATIENCE. It has never been off limits to our children. A comfortable two-seat sofa and a pair of lounge

BOOKCASE

A pair of French doors open to the entry area of the Settling Room. The doors are curtained on the far side so they can be closed down, but there are no locking doors into the Settling Room itself. Annabelle and I are the only ones in the house most of the time, and we don't feel the need for that level of privacy.

Though the Settling Room is on the far end of the house, it remains connected with a common thread of feeling. Both books and pictures form subtle but substantive ribbons between the extremities and the nucleus of the house.

Let me make one suggestion about books. Elegantly bound volumes aren't necessarily preferred over paperbacks. Paperbacks are less expensive, and they are easier to loan and use without worry of damage or loss. Don't limit yourself by thinking that there is just one right kind of book. Again, let logic and practicality guide you.

Shelves serve a unique purpose; they hold either books or other objects, but not both.

The small lamp in the bookcase does double duty. During the day, it casts a noticeably inviting glow into the natural shadow of the shelves. A low-wattage bulb also makes it an inexpensive but effective night-light.

MAX LUCADO
Riches Stored in
STRONG'S
ROMANS
Joy of Nature
THE WORLD'S GREAT RELIGIONS

chairs say that we're not in a hurry. We've always wanted the children to know that there is a place where we can draw aside and take time to work things through. Even Jesus had to occasionally draw away from the crowds and the hustle and bustle of ministry to take care of personal needs.

> Then Jesus said, "Let's get away from the crowds for a while and rest." There were so many people coming and going that Jesus and his apostles didn't even have time to eat. (Mark 6:31)

PATIENCE

Agreeably giving up my expectation of a speedy resolution to a difficult circumstance

Such interludes are vital, for they afford time to listen, time to pray, time to think. As we find ourselves trying to think through family needs, a place to get away is not a luxury.

Still, there is a tendency to put things off to a better time. After all, we reason, there's always tomorrow. Or is there?

In the early 1800s, missionary Adoniram Judson demonstrated his understanding of the profound significance of each day by writing these powerful words:

We have a general intention of living religion; but we intend to begin tomorrow or next year. The present moment we prefer giving to the world. "A little sleep, a little slumber." Well, a little more sleep, and we shall sleep in the grave. A few days, and our work will be done. And when it is once done, it is done to all eternity.

A life once spent is irrevocable. It will remain to be contemplated through eternity. If it be marked with sins, the marks will be indelible. If it has been a useless life, it can never be improved. Such it will stand forever and ever.

The same may be said of each day. When it is once past, it is gone forever. All the marks which we put upon it, it will exhibit forever. It will never become less true that such a day was spent in such a manner. . . . How shall we then wish to see each day marked with usefulness! It will then be too late to mend its appearance.

It is too late to mend the days that are past. The future is in our power. Let us, then, each morning, resolve to send the day into eternity in such a garb as we shall wish it to wear forever. And at night let us reflect that one more day is irrevocably gone, indelibly marked.[8]

Though each room in a house has its own purpose, there's something particularly unique about the Settling Room (and bedrooms in general). It's the last room we see at night and the first that we see in the morning. In a figurative sense, its usage can help us mark out our days—even emphasize the extreme importance of each one—as we greet both evening and morning there. "God called the light Day, and the darkness he called Night. And the evening and the morning were the first day" (Genesis 1:5, KJV).

From the standpoint of design, there are some practical considerations for the Settling Room. Other rooms (such as the Daily Room) are designed, furnished, and arranged with activity in mind. The Settling Room is not. Its design—from color scheme to furnishings to family accessibility—contemplates restfulness and quietness because the DISCERNMENT required to nourish family relationships requires such.

DISCERNMENT

The ability to separate cause and effect

It's a place where we can pursue relationships with each other, the family, and with God himself. Not much will happen without some quietness and unhurried solitude.

Though beauty is embodied in good design, I like to make houses as natural and normal as they can be. I don't want them to be so stiff that people ooh and ah but say, "That's nice, but I wouldn't want to live there." Good logic transcends rigid rules that don't work, and here are some concepts that I often run across.

Oddly, the most common request I get from men is "Get us soft carpeting to walk on barefooted in the master bedroom." And though I generally recommend that husbands allow their wives to make choices they (the husbands) don't fully understand, here is one place where wives can defer! Carpeting adds a warmth and sense of peace and quiet that enhances the settling atmosphere of the Settling Room.

[8]Adoniram Judson, letter to Miss Ann Hasseltine, 31 December 1810, *The Life of Adoniram Judson*, by Edward Judson (New York: Anson D. F. Randolf & Co., 1883). Republished in 1996 by the Institute in Basic Life Principles.

BED AND CHAIRS

The Settling Room has several types of specialized lighting. Overhead lighting can be dimmed to a candle-like radiance that flatters the room and illuminates son Kristian's artwork. Light from tall table lamps spills onto the bed for reading; if needed, they are supplemented by the spotlight projector above the bed. Some people prefer a separate spotlight—each with an independent switch—for each half of the bed. Though not seen here, soft night-lighting paves safe and silent transitions from bed to bath to closet.

On the bed itself, we use blanket covers and duvets or quilts that can actually be slept under. This avoids the extra bother of having to fold and store a bedcover whose only purpose is decorative.

Personal preference or medical needs will usually dictate one of two approaches to natural lighting: dark room or filtered light. Rooms can be almost completely darkened with blackout drape liners or shades, venetian blinds (preferably wood because they're so much nicer), or interior shutters.

For filtered light, good translucent unlined curtains allow some light without loss of privacy. Venetian blinds with the proper tilt also suggest a workable solution.

Throwing back all window coverings lets the entire room be awash with the outdoors when you need it!

In your desire for the perfect bedroom, don't act too quickly. I'm always grieved when I hear of young couples who have purchased a perfectly matched set of bedroom or dining-room furniture on credit. They'll be paying for three to five years, and they may not even like what they've done by then. I can't be more straightforward: Forget about purchasing matched sets. Mixing and matching is far more interesting, costs less, and accommodates genuine creativity.

Potential color schemes literally balloon with the mix-and-match route. What flexibility do you really have if bed, nightstands, triple dresser, lamps, and chest of drawers all match?

Personally, I feel that the woman of the house should have carte blanche when choosing the bedroom color scheme. Many men, for instance, initially fight the idea of floral fabrics, but once it's done, they ultimately not only approve but also eagerly share in the accolades from friends!

Some color schemes can't really be described. They have to be executed to be truly appreciated. My preference is for softer colorations that hint at a more romantic or settling feeling. Here are a few favorites:

- Butter yellow, pale jade green, pinks, and corals

SETTLING ROOM—COZY CORNER

If your bedroom is large enough (or if you can plan for new construction), try to eliminate the need for dressers and tall chests of drawers. Small bedside chests make a practical place to keep hosiery, underwear, and sleepwear. Relegating storage to well-organized closets or dressing areas will release more space to the bedroom itself.

We've tried to do this so our Settling Room can have a seating area. This allows Annabelle and me to casually and comfortably converse with our children, apprising each other of the day's events.

Other potential snarls to an otherwise well-planned bedroom can easily be avoided with a bit of forethought. The bookcase in this room resolves a common space-eating problem—the TV. Stereos with auxiliary speakers could be similarly handled. If there is space, a small stool or chair can eliminate the need for sitting on the bed to use the telephone.

- Blues and creams—Use many varied hues of blues, from turquoise to vivid cobalt, set against liberal doses of cream and ivory.
- Periwinkle blue and coral predominate our own Settling Room color scheme. These colors are separated with moldings of cream paint and set on a rug of cream sprinkled with a Maltese-cross design of the two aforementioned colors.

If you don't know what you really like, tour some homes and see if you can get just one good idea. Good design is simply a response to what you have been exposed to. If you see something done enough times, it will become a building block that you can further develop. All of this takes time, but that's part of the fun!

In following through with your plan, strive for a bedroom that's more than a bedroom. Aim for a real settling room where the real issues of life can be worked through.

A snippet from Thornton Wilder's famous play *Our Town* comes to mind. In it, Emily, who died in childbirth, is spending one day back among the living, where she longs to be seen and heard. Responding to her disappointment, Simon Stimson explains why no one notices.

> *Emily:* Oh, Mama, just look at me one minute as though you really saw me. . . . Do any human beings ever realize life while they live it?
>
> *Simon Stimson:* Yes, now you know. Now you know! That's what it was to be alive. To move about in a cloud of ignorance; to go up and down trampling on the feelings of those . . . of those about you. To spend and waste time as though you had a million years. To always be at the mercy of one self-centered passion or another.

How sad it will be if you assemble the perfect room but fail to listen, fail to care, fail to indelibly mark others' hearts by truly listening. Therefore, let us each resolve, as did Adoniram Judson, to send each day—while it is still called today—into eternity clothed with those instances of PATIENCE, kindness, DISCERNMENT, love, and tenderness that we would wish it to wear forever. There's no better place than the Settling Room to make and keep such resolutions.

7

The Hospitality Room

CHAPTER 7

THE MARKS UPON THE WALL

WITH BRUSH IN HAND, A ROOM TO PAINT,
BRIEFLY I DID HESITATE
TO SEE INSCRIBED WITH CHILDISH SCRAWL,
SOME PENCILED MARKS UPON A WALL.

AND THOUGH MY STROKES REMOVED EACH TRACE,
FROM MY MIND WAS NOT ERASED
THE CHILD WHO MADE THEM, GROWN TODAY,
IN THOSE MARKS WAS STILL AT PLAY.

AS PRECIOUS MEM'RIES FLOODED BY,
EACH RELIVED IN MY MIND'S EYE,
IT SEEMED TO ME THAT AFTER ALL,
WE EACH LEAVE MARKS UPON SOME WALL.

WHEN MY LIFE'S CANVAS IS WIPED CLEAN—
MY TIME HERE THEN BUT A DREAM—
WILL I HAVE LEFT SOME WORTHY MARKS
UPON THE WALLS OF OTHERS' HEARTS?[9]

Is there a greater legacy than having had a positive influence on others? We should yearn to leave our marks in such a way that those with whom our lives intersect will remember us for good. This is not a self-righteous wish; it's the same prayer twice uttered by godly Nehemiah, governor of ancient Judah: "Think upon me, my God, for good, according to all that I have done for this people" (Nehemiah 5:19, KJV).

Throughout the ages, one quality has been the hinge on which so much personal involvement with others has swung: HOSPITALITY. The Bible is filled with accounts of strangers who were compelled by hospitable people to share their food and lodging, as well as shelter and provender for animals.

[9]"The Marks upon the Wall" ©1996 James McAlister. Used by permission.

THE SERVING ISLAND

The serving island instantly identifies this room as the kitchen. When used as a setup area for a buffet, guests stand around it to give thanks before filling their plates and moving to a table, be it in the dining room or the breakfast room. Grandsons Calvin and Kent love to root around and mess up the cookbooks stored underneath, giving Granny something to do!

Note the windowsill at the sink; it's flush with the counter to give a totally unobstructed view of the outdoors. We can actually see out when seated.

The colors of the tiles on the wall below the kitchen cabinets are Annabelle's favorites: periwinkle, amethyst, and jade green. The tops of both the counters and serving island are surfaced with tiles containing a mix of these colors.

Other surfaces work well, too. You can use Corian, laminated wood, or a well-chosen shade of Formica laminate.

There are even different kinds of islands: working islands with range top and vegetable sink, serving islands, or table islands to sit at with stools or elevated chairs. Though some people try to mix the functions, the result is not always practical.

Though the basic idea is straightforward enough, there's an aura of mysterious importance embodied in HOSPITALITY. Its manifestation can unexpectedly commingle the human and divine in remarkable, life-changing ways. "Don't forget to show hospitality to strangers, for some who have done this have entertained angels without realizing it!" (Hebrews 13:2).

Abraham experienced this as he spontaneously entertained the three heavenly visitors who arrived without warning in the heat of the day (Genesis 18:1-5). On the other hand, Mary and Joseph were denied similar amenities in their time of need (Luke 2:4-7). What a blessing their potential hosts missed!

HOSPITALITY

Eagerly sharing the resources of my home to benefit others

We mistakenly presume that heavenly rewards are dispensed only in proportion to great outpourings of magnanimity and self-sacrifice. And while these are important, Jesus seems to highlight one-on-one commitments to the hungry, the naked, the sick, the stranger. He singularly but inextricably describes the exercise of HOSPITALITY toward the unlovely as a basis for his commendation. In that day of

HIDDEN WORKSTATION

Here is a strong indication that this room is the axis of the house. French doors that slide into "pocket reveals" open to expose the nuts and bolts of Annabelle's working day within the home. Clippings for the children—even at their advanced ages—correspondence, personal bookkeeping, planning for social engagements, and preparation of the outline of the day's events spring from this well-concealed, vital cubicle.

A major advantage of such an arrangement is obvious: the doors can be closed without having to take time to straighten up.

judgment, there may be surprises about who receives the greatest accolades.

> Then they will reply, "Lord, when did we ever see you hungry or thirsty or a stranger or naked or sick or in prison, and not help you?" And he will answer, "I assure you, when you refused to help the least of these my brothers and sisters, you were refusing to help me." (Matthew 25:44-45)

I must confess that I don't fully understand all that's implied here. But with a backdrop of such majestic import, shouldn't we evaluate how to involve ourselves in making a difference in others' lives?

Before the digital revolution, all watches had moving parts. While the malfunction of any single part could likely render the whole timepiece unusable, the mainspring was the prime mover. Without this part, the other gears, wheels, and springs were worthless.

To the extent that HOSPITALITY is the same kind of moving force in our homes, it *will* leave its mark. But what would be an appropriate genesis?

HOSPITALITY naturally emanates from the kitchen, or Hospitality Room. I still remember from childhood that certain homes in our

HOSPITALITY-ROOM DOORS AT WORK DESK

French doors with clear mirrors lighten and brighten a wall far more than solid wood doors can. Reflections of windows on the opposite side of the room create a striking window effect with a welcome airy openness.

Like so many spaces throughout the house, the serving counter to the right is filled with pictures. Mixtures of frame types and subjects reinforce the informal, comfortable atmosphere of this room.

neighborhood were known by all the kids as "Kool-Aid houses." No matter what the financial status, the kitchens of these homes were always delightful oases of refreshment and hospitality on the most basic level.

Even snacks and treats after church, a meeting, or other gatherings can be a simple entree. Many people go to a restaurant for this social time, but a home is far better. People can sense a spirit of GENEROSITY toward them that breaks down barriers.

GENEROSITY doesn't mean that we have to give away a lot of money, but it does include the attitude we have toward the possessions and resources under our control.

GENEROSITY

Not being stingy with resources that could be used to benefit others

Let me illustrate it this way. Annabelle and I once saw a film that made an indelible impression on us. In the opening scene, an overhead kitchen-cabinet door was opened, and a fine porcelain coffee cup plummeted to the floor, shattering into countless pieces. No ordinary cup, it was the last piece of porcelain in the family's heirloom dinner service.

CLOSE-UP OF DESK

Desks can serve many purposes, but few rival the intimacy of silent witness revealed here. Ever since our children were first able to read, Annabelle has placed clippings—the subjects vary from current events to Christendom to items of interest of a particular child—either on their beds or their bathroom mirrors.

"Paper the walls of the souls of your children." When I first heard these words, my heart was gripped and challenged as I recalled Annabelle's years of distributing simple bits of paper to the children. Surely these faithful works of her hands have left their marks for time and eternity.

YIDDISH HOUSE BLESSING

This house blessing was acquired through a newfound acquaintance who is involved in the Christian embassy in Jerusalem. Derived from the account of the Passover, these words from another culture and another time take on special significance as we say the blessing in the kitchen.

The blood shall be to you for a token upon the houses where ye are: and when I see the blood, I will pass over you, and the plague shall not be upon you to destroy you, when I smite the land of Egypt. (Exodus 12:13, KJV)

We have another blessing in our house as well. It's actually the prayer of a dear pastor friend offered at the dedication of our home.

Our Father and our God,

We thank Thee for our precious friends, Georg and Annabelle, and for their three lovely children and grandsons.

We thank Thee for their Christian testimony, not only throughout the area of Conway, but in many parts of the United States and of the world.

We thank Thee for the prosperity which Thou hast granted unto them and for their faithful stewardship of all that Thou hast entrusted into their hands.

We thank Thee for this beautiful and spacious house that you have given to them as a home for their family.

Now we pray thee, our Father, that Thou shalt sanctify this home to Thy use and for the ongoing of Thy Kingdom.

Bless Georg as the head of the family and priest of his own household. Give him wisdom and direction as he continues to lead his wife and his children in the ways of the Lord.

Bless Annabelle as the virtuous wife and mother of the home, and may she always be praised by her husband and children for the godly influence she brings to each life and each gathering in the home.

Bless the children—Katrina, Kristian, and Kirsten—their life's mates, and the children's children all the days of their lives.

Now, our Father, we do join with these loving friends to dedicate and consecrate this house—this home—to the cause and Kingdom of our Lord Jesus Christ.

In His name we pray, Amen.

BREAKFAST ROOM

The breakfast room is actually tucked off in a corner of the Hospitality Room, making the trip back to the serving island for more food an easy one.

By design, two doors open to allow interaction with guests in the Hospitality Room when two tables are required. Without rugs, concerns over spills are alleviated, and self-adhesive carpet glides on chair legs mitigate the possibility of scuffing the floor.

This room faces the front of the house where tall trees and shrubbery provide the "curtaining" needed for privacy.

Here's what touched us. That family had used its possessions—literally wearing them out—rather than relegating them to untouchable shelves until an ultimate, ignoble disposal by their heirs.

If we include others in our lives in such a way, our floors may get scuffed, our tabletops may be scratched, and our upholstery may be worn and faded. But should we worry about it? To me, these are tangible evidences of allowing a home to be broken and spilled out for others. Personally, I'd rather have my possessions be the first to wear down.

Our home is not used for anything on a big scale except to advance the kingdom, and I recognize my responsibility to be a good steward. Still, I want it to be thoroughly used without my being compulsive about my possessions. After all, who owns it all?

HOSPITALITY doesn't come easily. Having to consider the hurts and needs of others involves an additional burden that so many want to shrug off: "Cheerfully share your home with those who need a meal or a place to stay" (1 Peter 4:9).

GENTLENESS

The display of tender care and concern in reaching out to others

HOSPITALITY has a worthy ally in GENTLENESS.

What distinguishes a house from a home? All houses have walls and floors, but GENTLENESS sparks a nurturing and warm atmosphere. Who doesn't want to come to a home that provides a comfortable refuge?

During the first week of our marriage, Annabelle and I made a trip to the grocery store. When we came to the meat counter, she held up a large slab of meat, asking, "Honey, do you like this?" The same thing happened at the produce counter as I was queried about various vegetables. In each case, my unresponsiveness discouraged her. Why was I unresponsive?

CEILING CORNER DETAIL

In the breakfast room, periwinkle blue English ceiling paper is framed next to the crown molding with a hand-trimmed ivy-patterned border. Though the curtain fabric and wall covering do not match, they still tend to go together in this particular assemblage of color and pattern.

The periwinkle blue of the ceiling is reinforced with hand-loomed or woven periwinkle blue braid applied to the bottoms of the valances and front edge of the curtains.

Because when it comes to food, I am not visual until it is prepared and presented on my plate.

What's the point? Just this: even if I couldn't identify with what she was trying to do, I still could have been gentle and not shot her down at her every attempt to reach me. And while we might neither understand nor agree with all of those who come into our homes, GENTLENESS will not be out of place.

In designing our home, we gave a lot of thought to how we might increase our ability to be hospitable. For starters, we consulted a professional. Since the kitchen will be the most expensive room in the house, a professional who understands family—even your family—could probably help in getting the best use out of your investment.

Concepts of how a kitchen must be arranged are frequently archaic. With today's technology, new options are flowing into the marketplace in a steady stream. Even putting an oven next to the refrigerator is no longer taboo, and this can provide some interesting options.

Practically speaking, we've made the Hospitality Room a part of the Daily Room; there are no doors to seal off access between them. This was done to avoid the isolation that we felt in our last house. The opening between the two rooms is framed for French doors, however, should a future owner desire them.

We want guests to think of our home as an extension of their homes. Starting meals with prayer around the serving island in the kitchen puts them at ease. We then serve the food from

DETAIL OF BREAKFAST-ROOM TABLE

This table has a top of simple wooden planks. The "beaten-up" wood generates a ruggedly attractive patina that should not be hidden by a cloth.

The table requires no special care other than an occasional sponging!

there and encourage them to return to help themselves as many times as they wish. In a nutshell, we want to extend the reaches of our family.

I'm not a proponent of ecumenicism, but I do know that the time has come to build up the brethren. We must begin with the hospitality of our own homes to build up a good self-image in our mates, to encourage our children, and to love those whom we call brothers and sisters within the family of God.

The Ministry Room

CHAPTER 8

A DIFFERENT EYE

IN EARLY LIFE SHE OFT DID FALL,
SINS OF CRIMSON, KNOWN TO ALL.
CALLED A HARLOT (WHAT A SCOURGE),
MARKED FOREVER BY THAT WORD.

YET IN THE END GOD LIFTS HER HIGH;
WORKS BY FAITH DID JUSTIFY.
BY THAT FAITH MORE FRUIT HE'D BRING:
RAHAB'S LINE GAVE CHRIST THE KING.

THOUGH MEN HER LIFESTYLE MIGHT DECRY,
OUR GOD HAS A DIFFERENT EYE.
WE'RE RELUCTANT TO EMBRACE
THOSE WHO FALL IN SIN'S DISGRACE.

BUT GOD WHO SEES BEYOND WHAT SHOWS—
TO THE HEART THAT NO MAN KNOWS—
WITH DISCERNMENT IN THE END,
RECONCILED HER FAITH AND SIN.[10]

Why are we so reluctant to embrace those in need? Perhaps it's because we have a fear of being tainted and weighed down by their troubles. Or we may be repelled by the activities that brought on their current circumstances.

At the root level it may be even more simple—we just don't want to be bothered with someone else's problems. Seeing them through glazed eyes, however, has its consequences, and the joys, opportunities, and answered prayers that we stifle in the process are untold.

[10] "A Different Eye" © 1996 James McAlister. Used by permission.

To be effective in touching others, we must look beyond surface issues, perhaps even projecting our own frailties and vulnerabilities into their shoes. We need different eyes . . . eyes that speak of COMPASSION and TOLERANCE and HUMILITY.

In Bible times, having overnight guests was more the rule than the exception. Travelers could *depend* on having someone take them in for the night when they were on the road. But not today. A well-used guest room has such potential for meeting needs and healing hurts; for this reason we call ours the Ministry Room.

COMPASSION

Not withholding my resources to meet the needs of others

Consider the Shunemmite woman who often observed the prophet Elisha passing her house. Noting his situation, she first began to reach out by inviting him to share food with her family. But she didn't stop there.

> She said to her husband, "I am sure this man who stops in from time to time is a holy man of God. Let's make a little room for him on the roof and furnish it with a bed, a table, a chair, and a lamp. Then he will have a place to stay whenever he comes by." One day Elisha returned to Shunem, and he went up to his room to rest. (2 Kings 4:9-11)

She and her husband took that extra step and prepared a little room for Elisha whenever he might need it. Simply furnished, it met his basic needs. Still, it's not hard to imagine a few potential difficulties in such an arrangement; time really hasn't changed human nature that much. But the woman and her husband were willing to endure some inconveniences of the same sort that too easily put us off.

Elisha's schedule was unpredictable, and his arrival time was not known in advance. He just showed up . . . dirty . . . tired . . . lonely . . . discouraged. You name it. He may even have had other people with him. But the eye of the Shunemmite woman looked beyond the obstacles to a man with needs. She and her husband acted with COMPASSION to commit their time and resources.

HUMILITY

Giving up the right to make final decisions

MINISTRY ROOM—CLOSETS

There are two closets in this room; each has two doors for easy access. The first closet has racks for hanging clothes, while the other has only shelving.

There are no dressers in the room. This is purposeful, because almost all clothing that can be stored in a dresser can just as easily be put on shelves. This has an added benefit for travelers: It's harder to overlook items on shelves when packing to leave.

While I wouldn't go so far as to suggest that we should embrace *everyone* in need, whatever we choose to do must spring from HUMILITY.

Elisha's use of the little chamber was left to his discretion, and we must likewise hold our resources with a loosened grip.

Admittedly, the woman could see that Elisha was a godly man. Since that's not always the case, however, apprehensions may naturally arise. Certainly caution shouldn't be fully cast to the winds, but outward appearances don't begin to tell the full story. "Don't forget to show hospitality to strangers, for some who have done this have entertained angels without realizing it!" (Hebrews 13:2).

This verse is emphatically clear: Many who have reached out to strangers have unknowingly embraced angels instead. It's a sobering thought that such exciting encounters with heavenly messengers could be so easily missed.

Let me share an experience along those lines. We once invited two young men involved with Athletes in Action to stay in our home while they were in town for a speaking engagement. Strangers to us, they had arrived too late in the evening for us to become acquainted.

Our practice is to provide a very informal array of breakfast foods—cereal, fruit, bagels, and the like—that guests may access whenever they are ready. That removes the tension that can arise by forcing them to adhere to family schedules and tastes. Thus, these two men were already eating when I came in to visit before leaving for the worship service that morning.

When I told of how we had just recently learned of grandson Calvin's autism, one of the men was insistent: He must meet Calvin. A call to Calvin's father brought them both in a matter of minutes.

I'll never forget the young man's prayer that morning. With eloquence and sincerity, he implored his heavenly Father to let Calvin "touch the hem of Jesus' garment." The air was electric, and I sensed in an indescribable way that angels—the very ones who continually behold the Father's face—were permeating the room in ministry, both to Calvin and to us. What a privilege to have been there! But it could have been so easily missed.

MINISTRY ROOM—TOWARD THE BED

This is a hand-painted Mexican bed, a usable piece of art. Birds, flowers, and geometric patterns are painted to enhance its elaborate carved surface.

The bedcover is an unlined throw that guests can keep on the bed at night. Due to its informality and durability, taking a midafternoon nap on top of it causes no damage.

Floor-to-ceiling windows on three walls expand the room and almost make it a part of the outdoor gardens.

MINISTRY ROOM—TOWARD THE CHAISE

The off-white basket-weave upholstery is super-durable in spite of its coloration and the fragile connotation of its fiber—silk. Silk, as is the case with all natural fibers, is both strong and easy to care for. Wool, cotton, and linen fall into the same category.

Good lighting and a handy table surface for books or a laptop computer allow guests to steal away and work in comfort if they desire.

Keep artwork the same quality as in the rest of the house. Don't use your guest room as a graveyard for items that you don't really want. If you never liked Granny's old print, resist the temptation to foist it on your guests!

Our artwork is a broad mixture of types and media. None of it matches, but that gives so much more interest and flexibility. Our artwork includes

- *A favorite oil painting of a country lane that Annabelle chose years ago*
- *A painting by our son, Kristian*
- *An English antique-paper cutwork-framed floral*
- *Some of Annabelle's favorite needlepoint pillows*

Not all guests will be strangers; some may even be prominent. Busy people need to get away at times, so we try not to monopolize their time nor make them the center of attention. We've designed our home with that in mind, and our guests can generally come and go as they desire. Many have told us how much strain this alleviates.

In terms of design, our Ministry Room was planned to be near other critical areas of the house:

- The side entry for easy comings and goings
- The garage
- The laundry, in case it's needed
- The kitchen and pantry for snacks and breakfast, in case our schedules don't coincide with theirs

Our Ministry Room has its own bath, as do the children's bedrooms upstairs. We chose to have small baths so we could have more of them. In fact, we actually prefer it that way, and that's a practical trend that seems to be developing in home construction. Having large, luxurious baths may be nice, but there are usually fewer of them, causing people to have to wait their turn.

Since we are part-time empty nesters, each of the three children's bedrooms upstairs can serve as an additional Ministry Room if needed. One account is particularly memorable.

We were contacted by a friend who told us of a young couple under a burden of ministry-related stress. They needed some time away, and he wondered if they might stay at our home for a few days. The arrangements were made, and our upstairs bedrooms became the site of a very private three-day retreat that afforded them the rest and time together that they needed.

Not long afterward, we heard about some exciting consequences: In addition to having received rejuvenated attitudes, they were expecting their first child! We were grateful to have suffered whatever minor inconveniences most guests bring.

Regretfully, I am seeing guest rooms being de-emphasized. That's too bad, for it need not be that way. If necessary, guest rooms can be multi-purpose rooms, but I would offer a few

thoughts if you feel that you must take that route:

- If the room is a personal home office, there should be a way to secure personal files and other sensitive materials.
- Don't try to use a child's recreation room, an art studio, a craft room, or a sewing room as a guest room. A library or one-person sitting room will work much better. In any event, the room should be kept fastidiously clean and clutter free.
- The color scheme should be a direct reference to the the other colors in the house. If floral patterns are used, offset them with stripes and plaids to make men more comfortable.
- Two twin beds provide more flexibility than a double bed, and a portable alarm clock and a television are thoughtful provisions. You can also provide some reading material, but don't be didactic in your selections.
- If the room does not have its own bath, a freestanding towel rack with bath towels and facecloths lets your guests know which linens to use.
- Providing fruit and possibly a hot/cold thermos is a great idea for late arrivals.

TOLERANCE

Seeing others as "works in progress"

- An inexpensive luggage rack for your guest's suitcase is a handy item. In addition to convenience, it discourages placement of suitcases on the tops of furniture.
- A room can be personalized with thought-provoking mottoes or letters, framed and hung on the walls.
- We provide a guest book that we encourage our guests to sign.
- Don't cover every surface with fragile knick-knacks that are in constant peril of being knocked over.
- Depending on the season, a small fan or portable heater might be in order if the room is not individually zoned.
- Finally, try the room out yourself to see where it might fall short.

Having others share your home may bring some friction whenever different personalities rub together. An eye of TOLERANCE, however, will go a long way in not letting the immediate transgressions spoil the long-range view.

We are all in various stages of maturity and need to see one another that way. And when expectations go awry, there must be MEEKNESS to circumvent long-lasting hurt.

I'm trying to say that perspective and attitude are all-important in how we envision meeting others' needs. It would be marvelous if those to whom our homes are open could share these sentiments that Ludwig van Beethoven expressed to Emilie, a young pianist who had sent him a gift:

MEEKNESS

Not becoming angry when my expectations go unfulfilled

> I think I would rather visit you and your family than many wealthy people, in whom the poverty of their inner lives betrays itself. If ever I come to H., I will come to see you and your family; I acknowledge no other superiority in man save that which makes him take his place among really good people. Where I find such people, there is my home.[11]

May *we* be such people!

[11]Eva G. Conner, comp. *Letters to Children* (New York: Macmillan Company, 1938), 96.

The Banquet Room

CHAPTER 9

TODAY COULD BE THE VERY DAY

TODAY COULD BE THE VERY DAY
THE SKY ABOVE WILL BREAK AWAY,
REVEALING HEAVEN'S MAJESTY
OF STREETS OF GOLD AND CRYSTAL SEA.

CHRIST WILL DESCEND 'MIDST CLOUDS OF WHITE,
WITH ANGEL'S VOICE AND SHOUT OF MIGHT—
AS TRUMP OF GOD RESOUNDS ON HIGH—
IN JUST THE TWINKLE OF AN EYE.

THE DEAD IN CHRIST FROM EARTH THEN TORN
WILL MEET HIM IN THE AIR THAT MORN
ALONG WITH HIS WHO YET REMAIN,
INCORRUPTIBLE AND CHANGED.

NO SUN NOR MOON NOR DAY NOR NIGHT,
FOR GOD HIMSELF WILL BE OUR LIGHT.
WE'LL GET REWARDS FOR DEEDS DONE HERE
AND REIGN WITH CHRIST A THOUSAND YEARS.

IT SEEMS THAT TIME NOW MOVES SO SLOW,
BUT GOD THE DAY AND HOUR DOES KNOW
HE'LL CLOSE THIS AGE IN GRAND DISPLAY,
AND THIS COULD BE THE VERY DAY.[12]

For almost two millennia now, the time of Christ's coming has confounded experts' predictions. It's interesting that this singular event will not only culminate eons of anticipation but will also fling open the doors to the banquet of the ages—the wedding feast of the Lamb. Who would have thought that history's finale would be cast in a *banquet* scene?

In that day, rich and poor, young and old, healthy and infirm will be comfortably seated side by side. The parts they played in life will be forgotten, all at last on equal footing . . . and mutually sharing something significant—fellowship with each other and with Christ himself.

[12]"Today Could Be the Very Day" © 1996 James McAlister. Used by permission.

This glimpse of heavenly splendor and meaningful relationships should transform the mundane vision of dining room into one of Banquet Room! And what an exquisite pleasure it has been for us to anticipate that great day of the wedding feast by sharing "banquets of the heart" in *our* Banquet Room!

Let's set the stage with this premise: Effectiveness is determined by motive. If your goal in opening your home is to impress, others may be awed by the show, but one trip will more than suffice. They won't return. But a focus on serving will strike a resonant chord of intimate need.

ATTENTIVENESS

Shifting my focus to the needs of those who cross my path

Jesus himself placed a high value on serving others; that was one of his stated purposes in being here: "For even I, the Son of Man, came here not to be served but to serve others, and to give my life as a ransom for many" (Mark 10:45).

If serving is really your desire, you'll need ATTENTIVENESS to elevate your awareness of others' needs.

And remember that *all* have needs . . . even the "beautiful people" who seem to have it all together. Far too often the real needs are obscured by differing life goals or strains imposed by material status and social stratification.

BANQUET ROOM—OUTWARD GLANCE

This door's opening is not the full width of its architectural surround. We exploited this feature by building "half-butterfly shelving" to its left for some of Annabelle's favorite porcelain coffeepots and pitchers. The door is flanked by miniature wall cabinets for displaying special mementos.

How many should your table seat? Though ours seats twelve, I really think that eight is the ideal number. Conversation seems to be more enjoyable by all when there are eight or fewer.

Acoustics are frequently overlooked in a room's design. If the walls are painted or papered and the floors are bare or partially covered (as these are), you may want to give special attention to draperies.

Consider having draperies not only lined with cotton sateen but also interlined with flannel. This not only causes the fabric to hang better, but the flannel interlining adds soundproofing. Furthermore, the interlining blocks harsh light from coming through the fabric. The fabric's beauty is enhanced by having light shine on it rather than through it.

The Queen Anne–style hanging mirrors installed above the electrified sconces give added reflectivity and sparkle to the room.

You can't imagine—or maybe you can—the deep hurts that can come when someone purposely makes distinctions on the basis of physical appearance or station in life. We've had the unfortunate experience of having been "set aside," and scars remain.

In seeking to touch others, we must heed this strong admonition with pure motives:

> For instance, suppose someone comes into your meeting dressed in fancy clothes and expensive jewelry, and another comes in who is poor and dressed in shabby clothes. If you give special attention and a good seat to the rich person, but you say to the poor one, "You can stand over there, or else sit on the floor"—well, doesn't this discrimination show that you are guided by wrong motives? (James 2:2-4)

DISCRETION

Ordering my behavior so that it will not be offensive to others

In other words, you must be careful in your actions; DISCRETION must be uppermost in your thoughts.

There are a few practical steps that can avoid some subtle sources of offense.

Legend tells that King Arthur seated his knights at a round table to reduce quarrels over who might have the seats of greatest honor. Political protocol often relies on the same tactic to establish mutually agreeable ground.

Our Banquet Room has a large round table for similar reasons; guests are put more on the equal footing that we'll enjoy at the wedding feast of the Lamb. If we are using more than one table, there is no head table; family members are dispersed among the guests to avoid any appearance of preferential treatment.

Why go to the trouble of removing the status so often ascribed to seating positions? To facilitate the eye contact necessary for more intimate, meaningful conversation.

On a practical note, our eighty-four-inch table can comfortably seat twelve, but removing the leaves converts it into a sixty-inch size, more suitable for smaller numbers. We can even be effective with fewer guests by sitting together around one side. There's no benefit to being separated by an expanse.

Here's one situation where both DISCRETION *and* FLEXIBILITY would be crucial: You're expecting eight guests but find twelve at the door. What can you do?

When your motive is to meet needs, you'll suppress the natural despair that says "If I'd only known!" One of those extra people may need the evening most of all.

In seeking to reach out, stumbling blocks *will* pop up. But they are temporary and can be overcome with CREATIVITY.

If you have matched place settings for only eight, for example, quickly improvise. Fill in every third setting with another pattern, or mix and match if you have to. No one will ever know that you haven't set the table that way on purpose. Guests will likely marvel at the unique effect!

Are chairs a problem? Quietly go to your best friends—they are the ones who brought those extra guests—and ask *them* to compensate by sitting on stools, a piano bench, or whatever else may be handy. But *never* give the impression that your unexpected guests are an encumbrance.

Let's lay aside some presuppositions about what is required for a banquet of the heart by looking at two examples that are poles apart. Both thoroughly embrace others' inner needs but in vastly different ways.

Annabelle and I have friends in Nyack, New York, who are masters at making people feel welcome. For one week during the Christmas season, they go into the highways and byways giving engraved invitations to people—from friends to bag ladies to the down-and-out—for dinner in their home. We were invited one year.

This was no ordinary soup-and-salad affair. The table was gloriously arrayed with their best china, crystal, and cutwork tablecloth. Each plate was garnished with a bouquet of flowers that would satisfy any bride.

BANQUET ROOM—OVERVIEW

If you can, aim for a mixture of lighting types. Some should be overhead, via spotlights, a lantern, or other hanging fixture. This hanging lantern was chosen over a more elaborate chandelier.

Lighting from pin spots accents floral arrangements, the tabletop, and art around the room; lighting from sconces provides more of a gentle, flattering effect.

Both carpet and rugs (on wood or other hard surfaces) work well, and bare floors are especially pleasant in the summertime. If you use a rug, though, try to fit the table and all chairs on it. This rug's wrinkled appearance is intentional, a characteristic of Chinese handwork needlepoint rugs.

This photograph shows one of the more fun aspects of design. Our Banquet Room has four corner cabinets that give the room an octagonal shape, but one of them is actually a set of doors leading to the adjoining breakfast room.

The other three cabinets store and display various sets of china, glassware, and serving pieces. The pieces are placed in the cabinets in a rather utilitarian way, allowing Annabelle to use them with a minimum of difficulty. The cabinets' lower portions are paneled for storage of oversized serving pieces that are less frequently needed.

When some guests arrived, they were battered, tired, and worn out. But when they left, they had been revived and renewed during the nine formal courses of an exquisite meal prepared just for them. The evening was as remarkable as it is indescribable. Our friends plan for that week the entire year.

AVAILABILITY

Giving up my right to determine how my time and resources are spent

You certainly don't have to go to such an extreme to touch others, but there are times when that extra mile will leave indelible marks for good. On some occasions, paper plates and cups are adequate. Your AVAILABILITY is the key.

When you hold the resources at your disposal with an open hand, you'll get them back. And in abundance.

Be assured that poverty in possessions will be eclipsed by richness in the heart. A beautiful example is recounted in *By the Shores of Silver Lake* by Laura Ingalls Wilder. Her story encapsulates my feelings on "banquets of the heart" in a compelling way. Let me summarize a bit of it.

It was Christmas Eve, and the Ingalls family was snowbound . . . totally isolated from anyone else. Even if there had been money for

BANQUET ROOM—TABLE CLOSE-UP

If you have a table that is typically set up to hold ten to twelve chairs, but you'd like to use the room for four to six people, go ahead and do it. We frequently seat six using only half of our twelve-person table. For lunch, we orient the seating toward the windows; at night the hand-painted Chinese mural gets the focus.

There's no need to seat the host and hostess at opposite ends of the table. Cluster seating around one end is more functional and conducive to conversation.

My penchant for round tables lies in my desire to put all guests on equal footing. I also prefer using only side chairs. This removes the baronial feel and intimidation sometimes associated with particular seating arrangements.

The Banquet Room provides more opportunity than the other rooms for a bit of whimsy or fantasy. Color is particularly important, because food must look good. Apricots, French yellows, and all kinds of blues and beiges provide warmth and brilliance, while harsh whites and acid greens have just the opposite effect.

presents, there was no place to buy anything.

Even so, scraps of this and that were surreptitiously transformed: a bit of silk for a necktie for Pa and a piece of muslin for a dainty handkerchief for Ma. Old calico curtains became aprons, and the end of a worn-out blanket was made into bed shoes.

Eventually, everyone had a little something to open on Christmas morning. Then the unexpected happened: guests arrived!

ALERTNESS

An acute awareness of the significance of the times and circumstances in which I find myself

Mr. and Mrs. Boast were half frozen, their sled having been stuck and lost in the snow. Thawed by warm welcomes, they joyfully partook of a simple, hastily prepared fare of potatoes, gravy, and fried salt pork. Yet Mrs. Boast could not remember a meal that she had enjoyed more.

The meal was sufficient, but Ma's ALERTNESS noted one small problem that needed attention. There were no presents for Mr. and Mrs. Boast.

Laura was troubled by this, but Ma's attitude was calming. "Never mind, I'll manage somehow."

And she did. The next morning there was a present at each place at the table. Mrs. Boast

BANQUET ROOM—TEA SERVICE

The antique silver tea service (a generous gift from friends) sits on one of two tables where we store some of our flatware.

Some flatware is stored in the drawers of the serving buffet and two smaller tables. Since we tend to use the same flatware day in and day out, it makes more sense to keep it in the kitchen near the dishwasher.

The cutwork-lace curtain panels gently filter daylight and totally mask the black of the window glass in the evenings.

was delighted to have a gift, but what was it? Laura's heart leaped in surprise as soon as she saw it; Ma had given Mrs. Boast her best Sunday handkerchief.

Then Ma opened her package and put on the apron crafted in love. Inside the pocket was the fine muslin handkerchief that Mary and Laura had painstakingly made. Ma had willingly given her best handkerchief, only to unexpectedly be given another. It almost seemed planned, they thought, but it hadn't been.[13]

Daylight and dark don't do justice to the contrast. On the one hand, there's the elegance of the "Christmas house" with its nine-course meal, elaborate arrangements, and bouquets of flowers. A year's preparation is barely enough. Then there's the humble setting by the shores of Silver Lake. No thought of guests, barely enough food, sparse decorations, improvised gifts.

But both led to the same end: guests were touched by a generous outpouring of the best that was available. The best love, the best food, the best gifts. And "best" was not defined by material cost or quantity.

Do you *desire* banquets of the heart? If so, there need not be the feeling that they must be served in lavishness. It is, after all, a matter of the heart, and whatever material goods you have at your disposal will suffice.

Just *use* your Banquet Room . . . from the heart.

[13]Laura Ingalls Wilder, *By the Shores of Silver Lake* (New York: HarperCollins Publishers, Inc., 1939).

Come Again!

CHAPTER 10

JUST AN HOUR WOULD DO

TODAY I'VE MISSED SOME LOVED ONES
WHOM I'D LIKE TO SEE AGAIN,
TO FIX EACH FACE THAT TIME'S ERASED,
AND JUST AN HOUR WOULD DO.

FRIENDSHIPS KNITTED THROUGH THE YEARS
UNRAVELED BY DEATH'S TOUCH,
I'D TREASURE TIME TO RECOMBINE,
AND JUST AN HOUR WOULD DO.

I'D SETTLE FOR A MOMENT,
A BUBBLE IN THE STREAM
OF FLOWING DAYS AND SEVERED WAYS,
AND JUST AN HOUR WOULD DO.

TOMORROW CLOTHES THE PROMISE
THAT SEPARATIONS END,
AND HOLDS TODAY IN HOPE'S DELAY.
YES, JUST AN HOUR WOULD DO.[14]

Have you ever missed a person or a place so intently that "just an hour would do"? And to the longing heart, a brief reunion—even just an hour—would seemingly be salve enough for the moment.

When people leave your home and you bid them farewell with a "Come again," will they *sincerely* miss being there and *want* to return? And do you truly *relish* that thought?

The influence of your parting words at the door should be overshadowed by more important ones: the silent words that they should have heard and felt during their visit. This book has been about such words of silent witness.

[14]"Just an Hour Would Do" © 1998 James McAlister. Used by permission.

COME AGAIN—LOOKING OUT

The interior lighting has been kept low to balance the dusky exterior light. This lessens the contrast between bright interior illumination and the blackness of night.

"Well lighting" in the ground under the trees has been aimed upward. This prevents guests from being blinded by exterior floodlighting that is typically aimed toward the house.

Even if you have an honest, deep-rooted desire that your home extend its arms to embrace others, you can't compel your guests to come again. There must be something more binding: mutual investments in each other's lives. And while that will take time, there is a far more brilliant facet to the treasured gemstone of lasting relationships.

> There seems something else in life besides time, something which is measured not by minutes or hours, but by intensity, so that when we look at our past it does not stretch back evenly but piles up into a few notable pinnacles, and when we look at the future it seems sometimes a wall, sometimes a cloud, sometimes a sun, but never a chronological chart. Neither memory nor anticipation is much interested in Father Time, and all dreamers, artists and lovers are partially delivered from his tyranny . . . so daily life, whatever it may be really, is practically composed of two lives—the life in time and the life by values—and our conduct reveals a double allegiance. "I only saw her for five minutes, but it was worth it." There you have both allegiances in a single sentence.[15]

COME AGAIN—TOWARD REAR PATIOS

Overscaled Adirondack chairs are clustered throughout the property, providing a subtle invitation for guests to sit and linger a bit before going back home.

[15]E. M. Forster, *Aspects of the Novel* (New York: Harcourt, Brace and Company, 1927).

Would others call a visit to your home one of the "notable pinnacles" of their lives? A pinnacle not gauged by clock or calendar but by

the intense *quality* of the encounter?

Will your guests have sensed that touching others is more than a passing vapor in your life? Will they know that you want to be friends as well as friendly? Will they have departed with a bolstered self-worth? Will they be haunted by a

lingering conviction that your home's last word and first word are both ANTICIPATION?

If so, they will want to return without compulsion, and "Come again" won't even be necessary. But say it anyway.

COME AGAIN—TOWARD GARDEN WALL

Chair groupings actually define outdoor "rooms." This room is a playroom, always equipped with toys for children to use and enjoy.

JAMES McALISTER

James McAlister graduated from the University of Arkansas in Fayetteville with degrees in electrical engineering and is a registered professional engineer. He began writing freelance articles for technical magazines in 1970 and has published scores of them on topics that vary from computers to personal development to religion. Some articles have won awards, and many have been reprinted in a variety of encyclopedia volumes.

Coincident with his daughter Jenny's death in 1995, he began writing poetry, including all the poems in this volume. Members of the church that he attends have set other poems to music for congregational singing. His long association with the character-based teachings and ministry of the Institute in Basic Life Principles has provided the background for writing the definitions of the "words of silent witness" that express the character of the home. He also self-syndicates a newspaper column that focuses on character-related issues.

Mr. McAlister and his wife of 32 years, Mary Winborn McAlister, make their home in Conway, Arkansas, with their 18-year-old son, Barrett. His e-mail address is jmc@ieee.org.

GEORG ANDERSEN

Georg Andersen, ASID, is an interior designer extraordinaire. A native of Long Island, New York, he graduated in 1961 from Parsons School of Design (an affiliate of New York University), New York City, where he later taught interior and architectural design. Upon graduation from Parsons, he attended L'Ecole de Architectur, Fontainebleau, France, on an ASID full scholarship.

He was awarded the Hexter National Design competition's First Honorable Designer of the Year Award. The International Hotel/Motel and Restaurant Association awarded him the Gold Key Award for excellence in interior design, presented by Mr. Henry Kissinger. Mr. Andersen is also a five-time ASID Gold Award recipient.

He has been featured in all major architectural and interior-design publications, including *Architectural Digest,* and has appeared on major television networks, including CBS, NBC, and ABC. He has provided design services to such clients as the Waldorf-Astoria Hotel in New York City, the White House (Kennedy administration), Glen Oaks Country Club on Long Island, and many others, often controlling the design of the landscape architecture as well.

Georg Andersen Associates, Inc., has its headquarters in Conway, Arkansas, and also maintains offices in New York City. Georg currently makes his home in Conway with his wife, Annabelle.

GLOSSARY OF TERMS

ALERTNESS An acute awareness of the significance of the times and circumstances in which I find myself

ANTICIPATION The eager expectation that God's promises are true and that he will work through my circumstances to fulfill them

ATTENTIVENESS Shifting my focus to the needs of those who cross my path

AVAILABILITY Giving up my right to determine how my time and resources are spent

BOLDNESS The confidence that neither my words nor my actions are morally offensive to God or to others

COMPASSION Not withholding my resources to meet the needs of others

CONCERN Displaying sincere attention to the needs of others

CONTENTMENT Accepting God's present provision of shelter and clothing as sufficient

CREATIVITY Seeing new ways to get around the roadblocks to achievement

DISCERNMENT The ability to separate cause and effect

DISCRETION Ordering my behavior so that it will not be offensive to others

ENDURANCE Withstanding life's trials until God's work has been accomplished

ENTHUSIASM The outward expression of the joy that is in my heart

FAITH Visualizing God's plan for me and responding accordingly

FLEXIBILITY Not being rigid in my approach to achieving my goals

GENEROSITY Not being stingy with resources that could be used to benefit others

GENTLENESS The display of tender care and concern in reaching out to others

GRATEFULNESS A thankful response to the benefits that have come into my life

HOSPITALITY Eagerly sharing the resources of my home to benefit others

HUMILITY Giving up the right to make final decisions

LOYALTY Maintaining faithfulness to God and others, even during trying times

MEEKNESS Not becoming angry when my expectations go unfulfilled

ORDERLINESS Arranging my surroundings to maximize their usefulness

PATIENCE Agreeably giving up my expectation of a speedy resolution to a difficult circumstance

RESOURCEFULNESS Making the most of the resources available to me

REVERENCE Acknowledgment that God is always at work to mold me into the image of Christ

SENSITIVITY Perceiving the real needs of those with whom I have contact

SINCERITY The genuine, earnest desire to help others without the motive of personal gain

THRIFTINESS Avoiding unnecessary expenditures

TOLERANCE Seeing others as "works in progress"

INDEX

The Carlyle Hotel, New York, New York The Waldorf-Astoria, New York, New
York, New York The Mayfair Regency, New York, New York The Drake Hote
Churchill Hotel, London, England Round Hill Hotel, Montego Bay, Jamaica
New York, New York Peacock Alley at the Waldorf-Astoria Hotel, New York,
York The Hampshire House Restaurant, New York, New York LePavillon, Rit
The Omni, Atlanta, Georgia The French Restaurant, The Omni, Atlanta, Ge
York, New York Banco de Estado de Brazil, New York, New York La Banc Co
and Trust Company, Tupelo, Mississippi Deposit Guaranty Bank, Tupelo, M
Mississippi First State Bank, Lonoke, Arkansas Bristol-Meyers Company,
Phelps Dodge Corporation, New York, New York Rockwell International, At
York, New York Gelberg & Abrams Law Firm, New York, New York Gulf Towe
Systematics, Inc., Little Rock, Arkansas Kimberly Clark, Conway, Arkansas
Arkansas Charles Sutton Reproductions, Winston/Salem, North Carolina J
Regional Hospital, Conway, Arkansas Baxter General Hospital, Mountain
Memorial Hospital, Spartanburg, South Carolina John L. McClellan Memo
Hot Springs, Arkansas Palmetto General Hospital, Hialeah, Florida Vetera
Towers, Little Rock, Arkansas Neurology Associates, Little Rock, Arkansa
Retirement Center, Little Rock, Arkansas Norwegian Home, Brooklyn, New
York The Carl Stuart Middle School, Conway, Arkansas Marguerite Vann E
Arkansas University of Central Arkansas, Conway, Arkansas SNU, Bethany, C
Rhinebeck, New York Franklin Avenue Baptist Church, Malverne, New York
Arkansas Second Baptist Church, Conway, Arkansas St. Joseph Catholic Chu
Glen Oaks Country Club, Long Island, New York The Metropolis Country
Walton Fine Arts Center, Fayetteville, Arkansas The White House, Diplomati
The Governor's Office, Arkansas State Capitol Building Aspen, Colorado
California Fairfield, Connecticut Fayetteville, Arkansas 800 Fifth Avenue,
York, New York 855 Fifth Avenue, New York, New York 857 Fifth Avenue, N
York, New York 1080 Fifth Avenue, New York, New York 575 Park Avenue,
York, New York 785 Park Avenue, New York, New York 1070 Park Avenue,
New York, New York The Carlyle Apartments, Madison Avenue, New York, N
York, New York 870 United Nations Plaza, New York, New York Greenwic
(private palace) Hot Springs, Arkansas Kansas City, Missouri Little Rock, A
Santa Fe, California San Diego, California Springdale, Arkansas Stratton,
County, New York (more than 100 residences) A&E Stores, New York, New
Kahn Jewelers, Hot Springs, Arkansas Kahn's Jewelers, Pine Bluff, Arkansas
Stores, New York, New York (five stores) Zoldan Equities, Westchester,